MY FATHER'S SHOES
Life Stories and Other Memories

Raymond F. Vennare

Front and back cover photos: Annie O'Neill
Book design: Michael Kainaroi

Print ISBN: 978-0-7867-5500-4
ebook ISBN: 978-0-7867-5501-1

Distributed by Argo Navis Author Services

Distributed by
Argo Navis Author Services
www.argonavisdigital.com

CONTENTS

FOR MY FATHER

Just before my father died I bent to kiss his forehead. And as I did his fading heart slowly ceased to beat. As he exhaled his final breath, I inhaled and took him in, so that the life that left his body would live in me forever. I am twice born to my father, once in birth and once in death.

RFV

ACKNOWLEDGEMENTS

Books don't write themselves and authors are merely a conduit between personal expression and shared experience. Everything else required to produce, publish and distribute a book requires knowledge, experience and expertise. I lack all of these.

My Father's Shoes simply would not exist without the support – menial, manual and moral – of my family, friends and colleagues. It exists because of the hard work of many talented people.

I owe the inspiration for this work, first and foremost, to my family. My brothers Alfred, John and Paul. My sister Roseanne. My paternal grandparents Pasquale Vennare and Stella Bellina Cerra. My maternal grandparents, Giovanni Dabecco and Roseantonia Bruno. Most especially, of course, I owe my very existence to my mother Isabel Rose Dabecco, and my father Alfred Michael Vennare, to whom this book is dedicated.

To Cynthia, the first agent to give me the time of day, if not my first reality-check, I thank you. To Lillie, a dear friend and an author and mentor in her own right, I appreciate your generosity of spirit and willingness to share. To Frank, your tenacity, integrity and passion have lifted and inspired me. To La Famiglia – Mary Del and Richard, Pete and Kate, Pete and Regina, Carole and David – you are the family I have chosen and the people I admire. But more than any other person, to Cally, for never once wavering in her encouragement, faith and support, nor questioning my need to write this memoir.

There are a host of others who have read, re-read and commented on various chapters and story selection. A few are now helping me write Senza Memoria, a play based upon these stories. Others have helped shape the design, content and persona of the book.

You know who you are and I thank you all from the bottom of my heart.

INTRODUCTION

This book has evolved over time. The manuscript was initially written as a Christmas gift to my father. The original title, now the subtitle was, "Life Stories and Other Memories".

I wanted to share certain memories with my father that were meaningful and lasting. And I wanted him to know, from my perspective, just how important he was in my life. He never really understood the profound impact that he had on the lives of other people – especially his family. Because of that humility, or perhaps in honor of it, I wanted to him know, in no uncertain terms, that he truly made a difference in this world.

As others read the manuscript they seemed to recognize something of themselves in these stories. A memory. A passage. An incident or feeling. As they did I became comfortable with sharing, more openly, these vignettes of family life.

In the end this book is really more about me than my father. But, even more than that, it is about appreciating every circumstance in life however mundane or unremarkable it may seem at the time. These seemingly discrete and unrelated moments actually define who you are, what you become and what matters most in life. At least they did for me.

My Father's Shoes is, at its core, an anthology of short stories. The book is allegoric and the shoes are metaphoric. Unlike most anthologies, however, these stories are an amalgam of themselves. They integrate and coalesce. There is a rhythm and a cadence both in substance and in form.

My father always used to say, *senza memoria vita non esiste*, which in Italian means, 'without memory life does not exist'. These are my memories and this is my inheritance. These memories are either rooted in personal experience or derived from stories that were entrusted by a father to his son. As much a compilation of oral history as living history these stories and the people in them are real. While the passage of time may have inadvertently eroded the accuracy of certain inconsequential details, some names have been deliberately changed, or timelines compressed, for purposes of anonymity, emphasis or continuity.

CHAPTER 1

MY FATHER'S SHOES

I came upon a photograph that I had never seen before. Black and white and brown and yellow and chipped along the edge. Slightly worn and somewhat faded but well preserved for many years. It was in a box with other boxes. And in each box a bag. And in each bag were envelopes that were dated year-by-year. Every packet was a person. Every envelope a life.

It was the Class of 1941 at Beechwood Elementary. I recognized the entrance to the building where they stood. I could see that it was winter by the snow and ice and frost. It was cold and it was overcast on Rockland Avenue. The photographer had cleared the steps with a shovel and a broom and he used the stairs as risers to arrange them each by height. Three rows deep of thirty-one. Fifteen girls and sixteen boys.

I attended Beechwood School in 1958 and the teacher of my father became my teacher too. Her name was Ruth Ann Griffiths-Buete and she taught for several decades. Miss Wagner did. Miss Citron too. Miss Zaringer came later.

Joseph Bahr had been the principal as long as anyone remembered and Mrs. Ruch, who taught us music, played viola and piano. She would tell us that her father played the piccolo and flute. That he had marched in step for fifteen years with Susa's famous band. There was a sense of continuity from one decade to the next. A sense of obligation by the father to the son. The teachers knew the children-of-the-children they had tutored and the children knew the teachers by their parents' education.

There always seemed to be a link. A common binding thread. The link was that our fathers or our mothers had preceded and the teachers were the common thread that bound us all together. The teachers were our mentors. They were respected and admired. And my father made it very clear that Beechwood was a gift. And it felt like an inheritance when they passed it on to us.

Every person in that picture, which had been taken on that day, signed the back of that memento with their name in pen and ink. The blue and black of fountain pens bled sepia and brown. The ink had faded, pale and blurred, but the names had all survived. Thomas Jones and Clara Davis. Tony Gimigliano. Edward Falvo. Robert Lamb and Donald R. McClendon. William Gianopulos. Patsy Hartman. Milton Jackson. Dorothy Bulford. Olive Peach and Katherine Donaldson. All the names were neatly penned and carefully arranged. They were indelible and lasting. They withstood the test of time.

Shuffling through these memories, like Solitaire or Hearts, the people and the places and the memories came back. Some have long since passed away. Some are very much alive. Some were men I never knew. Some were women who have died. It was a thirty-minute journey through eighty years of life. It was joyful if unbearable to remember who they were. But in that timeless faded photograph, in that image of a boy, I came to know my father and my father's son as well.

The photograph was sobering. It was a jarring confirmation. It reminded me of moments that had long since passed me by. Moments full of meaning that were yet to be revealed. Not then at least. But now I do. And I remember more each day. Much I had forgotten or had simply never known. But there it was in front of me and now I understand.

The shoes of all things made me cry. Heavy, brown and worn. Scuffed and frayed and weathered shoes that were neatly laced and tied. They were an eloquent reminder of the life that he was living. A metaphor. A simile. A symbolic affirmation. My father's shoes were different than the shoes the others wore. They matched the earth beneath his feet. Not the suit that he was wearing.

And what a man these shoes have filled. Shoes that I will never fill. Immigrant. American. The youngest of thirteen. Ten of them including him survived beyond their birth. I never knew his mother. I was born six months too late. She had died in January. I was born in June. But I have always felt a kinship not so easily explained. As if my birth was planned by God to compensate her death. My father loved her very much, and it crushed him when she died, so I always thought that I was born to fill that void for him.

His father I knew very well and I miss even now. He always smiled and rarely cursed and he never raised his hand. My father was a tailor's son. And the tailor was like him. A gentleman with dignity. A family man with pride.

By the time that this old tailor's son was brought into this world little more was given him than love and work and faith. His clothes were mostly hand-me-downs. Stitched and sewn and dyed. Borrowed suits that never fit from brothers twice his size. He went to school in threadbare pants that were patched, if well concealed, but for all the things he could not have the shoes at least were his. He chose them well. He wore them well. They lasted many years. They had to last. They had to fit. He had no other shoes.

I wish that I had been there when he was growing up. To talk with him. To be his friend. To share that life with him. To live the life that shaped my life before my life had come. Unfortunate in many ways but simple and complete. Struggle and uncertainty were with him every day.

But survival has its own reward that survivors only know. They are the moments in a lifetime that can make or break a man. They are choices born of fate or fear. They are convictions of the soul. And the life whose moments made this man made him thoughtful and assured. Cautious but deliberate. Precise in every way. He worked hard and he worked often and he worked to get ahead. He worked his way through poverty, adversity and war. He worked his way through college and through marriage and through sorrow. He worked his way through illness and through sadness and through pain.

His triumph over circumstance made him see life very clearly. The importance of the family and the value of a conscience. Simple things. Essential things. And they didn't cost a dime. They were words or they were gestures. A prayer. A laugh. A tear. A firm embrace. A gentle touch. A glass of wine with dinner. Our family and our dignity meant more to him than gold. So integrity and honesty were nurtured in our home. These were things that no one else could ever take away. And this is what my father taught as it was taught to him.

My father felt another's pain more deeply than his own. It touched him and affected him in ways I'll never know. Others. Always others. Stranger. Family. Friend. He lived to make the lives he touched far better than his own. It shaped him and it changed him and he asked nothing in return. He gave away what mattered most. His heart. His hopes. His dreams. And what had not been freely given others tried to take away. All of this I'm certain was the conscience of his youth. The time he lived. The life he lived. The people and the place. An experience of living that can never be replaced.

The neighborhood where I grew up is where my father's father lived. They settled there from Italy. Before the ravages of war. Like Beechwood School our neighborhood was buried in tradition. It paid homage to our parents and we felt like we belonged. It was a synthesis of many but a community of one. It was a logical extension of the family and the home. Where parents cared and children played and friendships formed at birth. Door-by-door and house-by-house that neighborhood was ours.

When the immigrants had first arrived they settled on The Hill. They lived in shanties or in tenements. They lived in hovels or in tents. They moved to Oakland in the Hollow. Or to Larimer or Wylie. They tried to build a whole new life. They yearned to be accepted. They asked for nothing more than fairness but some would lose more than they gained. So they understood the need to share. To help those most in need. To preserve their ways and still fit in but never to give up.

Their lives were bound together like the teacher to the pupil. There was a common thread of circumstance. Of providence and fate. They understood the concept of the whole and of its parts. They were proud of what together they could not achieve alone. But what a life they must have lived. Regardless of their calling. When fraternity meant something more than hazing and a pin.

Some of this comes back to me. Those moments as a child. When I was young and they were old and I was witness to tradition. I saw it as they lived it. I knew their ways first-hand. But I wondered then, as I do now, if their lives were any better. Was it better than their homeland that had forced them into exile or worse for having made the choice to reinvent themselves? Was it the land of opportunity that so many had imagined or a land of opportunists who took advantage of their plight?

On the backs of faceless immigrants rode industry and commerce. They carried hods of brick and mortar. They worked the coalmines and the steel mills. They built homes in which they could not live and schools they could not enter. They died in caves and furnace rooms for fifty-bucks a month, and perished for the dreams they dreamt, persevering as they struggled. The depression had deprived them of their dream of *abundanza* and abundance was the very thing that brought those people here. They heard about this country, and the riches that it offered, and they dared to leave their families and the little that they owned. But the poverty from which they came in

Appeninio Calabrese was in many ways far better than the terror that they faced. Proud and humble workingmen brought slowly to their knees. They were family men and husbands who were desperate to succeed.

And if not for all the women, often stronger than the men, the neighborhoods and families may never have survived. The unity and power of a communal act of living was in the hands of gentle women who were hardened by their plight. In the absence of what others saw as basic human rights the women of the neighborhood invented family life. And the voice of those who struggled still echoes in those streets. In the bricks and in the mortar. In the sidewalks and the walls. In the lives of those who carried on. The descendants of those dreamers.

Every brick and every stone, and every piece of glass, was cut or chipped or carved or laid to make some dream come true. Not for them but for their children. And for their children's children too. These streets are where my father walked and where my mother carried me. As did their sisters and their brothers and their fathers and their aunts. Where they would stroll and point and name those things that have meaning to me now.

Because of them – the family, the neighborhood and friends – that place is now a monument that still honors them today. It provides a sense of being and a sense of having been. It protects our true identity. It justifies our name. Not just the house that we called home. But the neighborhood as well. The markets and the corner shops. The sidewalks and the parks. The churches and the trolley cars. The pool hall and the bars. They belonged to all of us and we belonged to them. It was a simple rite of passage to have grown up in this way. To take our place in place of those who made that place our own. It was the people not the brick facades. The voice inside the door. The friends we buried in the ground whose names we knew so well. It was the experience of living there that unified us all.

It's been eighty years, or maybe more, since that neighborhood began. But to this day when I pass by, and meet the son-of-some-one's-son, they will start the conversation by appreciating that they knew my father or my mother or my uncle or aunt. They grab my hand and shake it. They look me in the eye. They know that when they do this they are reaching back in time. It binds me and it ties me to my family and my home. To the people on their porches. To the friend-ships and the food. To the dreams of all those dreamers who had built that neighborhood.

When I thought about my father's shoes, in that faded photo-graph, all of this came back to me and now I love him even more. The shoes he wore spoke volumes. They told the story of his life. Of his birth and of my birthright. Of the struggle of his years. I know now what he knew then. What he forever kept inside. Like his shoes, and like his life, he had nothing else to wear. He chose them well, and wore them well, and I am humbled by his life.

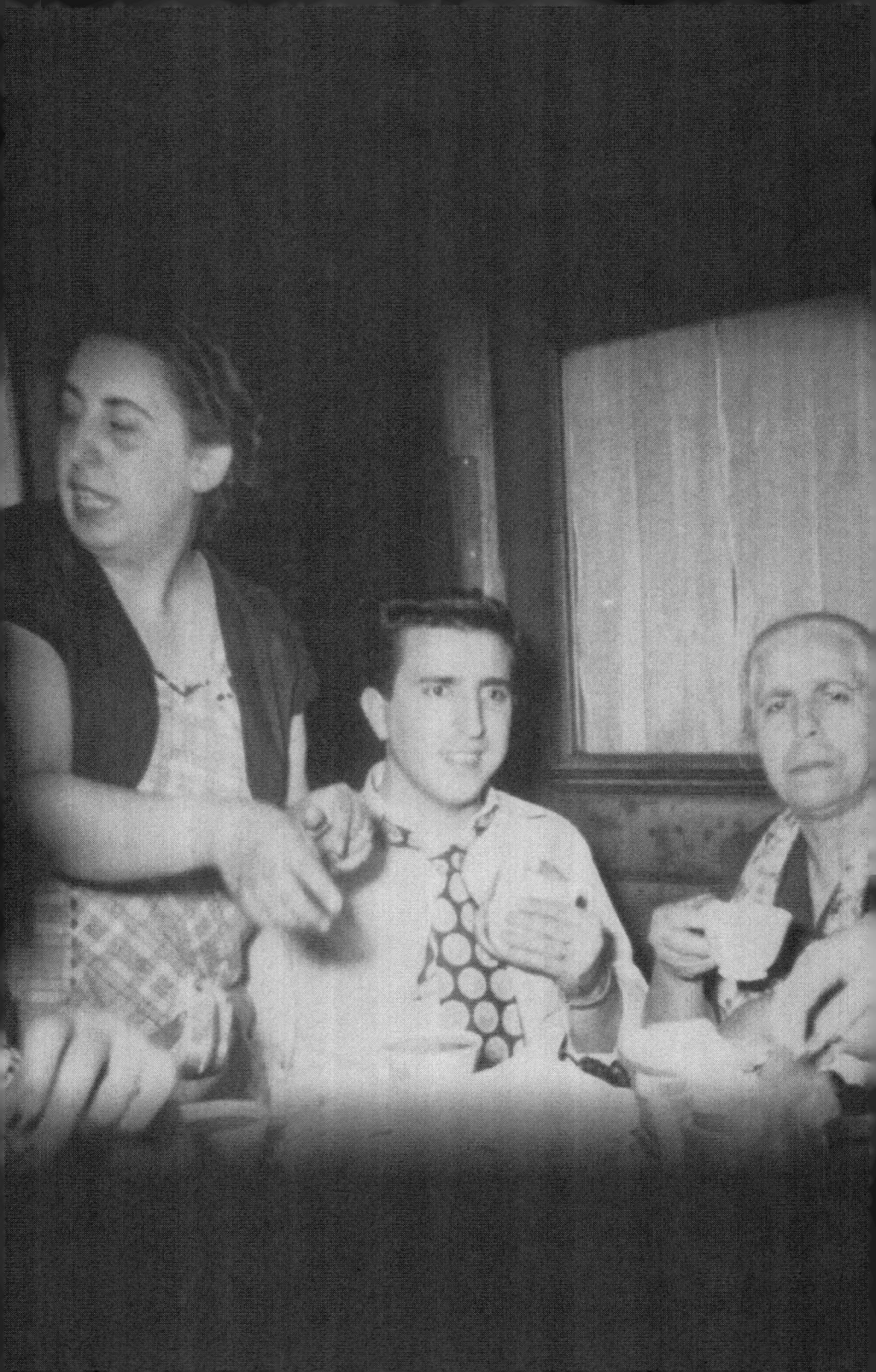

CHAPTER 2
THE TABLE

The table was a sacred place. It was the center of our being. And everything that happened there would change our lives forever. It was our cosmos and our universe. It was our sacrificial alter. It was the Temple of the Progeny. Our confessional. Our chapel. It was the setting of our daily meals, however frugal or abundant, and we recognized the purpose and the meaning that it had. It was the starting point and resting place of every single day. It was the only time when we were whole and gathered all as one.

It could be a workbench or a study hall. A clubhouse or a crib. Where Easter eggs were dipped and dyed and pumpkin heads were carved. Where repairs were made to everything from a lampshade to a toaster and model planes and boats and cars were molded, glued and crafted. Homes were dreamed and gardens planned and marriages arranged. Newborns named and deaths announced around the family table. Life oozed from every slat and nail and plank and board and screw. The table was symbolic of the love that we all shared.

The shape and size would change at times responding to our needs. The length would change. The width would change. It was rectangular or round. It was square or it was oblong. It was long or it was short. But whatever shape or size it was it fit us like a glove. We used wooden chairs and metal chairs and folding chairs and benches. We used cushioned chairs and hard-backed chairs and high-backed chairs and couches. Anything and everything that we could use to sit we would pull up to the table and we would make a meal of it.

CHAPTER 2

My favorite was the picnic bench. Big and red and deep. With redwood slats and two-by-fours that were tightly nailed together. My father had to broaden and extend it at both ends. He had to make it functional and durable and large. He made it wide enough and long enough and strong enough and sturdy for all the weight of cast iron pots and metal pans and platters. But even so the table strained to support the daily meals. It bowed beneath the heaviness and dipped from end-to-end.

The food and forks and bowls and plates, the glasses and the baskets, were stacked and squeezed and pushed and shoved and made to fit that space.

Isabel, my mother, served us family style. Italian. Simple food and modest meals but filling and delicious. Homemade cooking. Hand made meal. Morning, noon and night. Every day. Three times a day. Seven days a week. She would transform the basement kitchen into a lavish banquet hall by the quantity and frequency of everything she made.

It was culinary magic. Gastronomic hocus pocus. Merlin found his equal in my mother at the stove. At first glance there was nothing but a bare and empty table. Then look again and *presto*. A table stacked with food. It poured from every bowl and tray or pot or pan or saucer. Enough to feed each hungry mouth sat drooling on the bench. Ten of us were served like this for breakfast, lunch and dinner. Seven kids and three adults. Two parakeets. Two dogs.

But Sunday was the real event. The fishes and the loaves. When platoons of faithful followers routinely joined our ranks. The parents of my mother or the brothers of my dad. Sisters. Uncles. Cousins. Aunts. An unexpected friend. A relative from out of town. A kid from down the block. She never knew how many but she always made enough. It was a miracle, not magic, because it wasn't sleight of hand. And she did this every Sunday. Every week of every year.

From just one pot or pan or plate an army had been fed with fresh baked bread and homemade soup and pasta by the pound. We picked the lettuce and tomatoes and the onions from the garden and tossed them in a salad bowl with a wooden fork and spoon. We drank *espresso* by the gallon. We ate *biscotti* by the dozen. We cut peaches and *castagna* nuts and soaked them all in wine.

My mother's meals were marvelous. They were delicious and harmonic. She was a *maestro* at the podium. Toscanini with a spoon. She knew when food was sharp or flat with garlic, salt or basil and instinctively she paused between the courses that she served. She conducted every movement with a ladle or a fork. She would rest between each helping of the pasta and the soup.

The leitmotif of every meal was the flavor and the texture and the taste of all that homespun food was seasoned with her love. It was peppered with tradition and salted with a prayer and we begged like little homeless waifs in a Charles Dickens novel. We pawed and grabbed and poked and groped with our stubbly little fingers. We pushed and pulled and shoved and nudged to claim our rightful place.

We climbed across the table for *polenta* or *lasagna* or a piece of hot *salciccia* or *focaccia* or *bruschetta*. Tearing at the loaves of bread that blessed our daily table we would dip it in the drippings of the chicken *cacciatore*. Or we brushed it with some oil, or oregano or garlic, and we toasted it and showered it with imported *parmigiana*.

Food was lifted, passed or pilfered as it moved across the table like a levitating spirit at a séance for Houdini. Up-and-down and back-and-forth from the platter to the plate we had one hand on the *penne* and the other on *vitello*. A fork was in the *fritti* and a spoon was in the *zuppa*. It was "pass me this" or "give me that" or "I want some *melanzane*." It was absolute insanity. It was chaos. It was love.

The background to this simple feast of farina, bran and flour was the lively animation and the laughter that we shared. There was syncopated slurping and bilingual conversation. And, like the salad and the croutons and the sharp imported cheese, English and Italian were tossed and mixed and crisp. It was loud and it was lively. It was *fortissimo profondo*. It was atonal and chromatic and it was music to my ears.

Between the passing of the butter and the breaking of the bread was the clinking of the glasses and the popping of a cork. Wine was poured and sipped and served, with almonds, figs and dates, and augmented or diminished by incessant conversation. There was no etiquette to speak of when we were talking at the table. Spontaneous eruptions were more than commonplace. We had protagonists and allies. We had tattle-tales and spies. But arguments were strictly banned until the coffee had been served. Ideally we were taught to be considerate of others. Especially our family and our elders and our friends. We were expected to be courteous and patient and attentive. To wait our turn before we spoke. To speak when spoken-to.

In practice though it never worked. We were too hyper and spasmodic. Not that we were crude or rude. Just vying for attention. If my father asked a question during dinner at the table then every single one of us would tell him what we thought. All of us. In tandem. Seven children spoke their mind.

It reminded me of wrestling with Bruno Samartino or Jumping John DeFazio or Whipper Billy Watson. We were the midget tag-team sideshow, not the main attraction, with tiny little arms and legs flailing at the table. We were pleading to be noticed. We were sucking-up to dad. We were looking for approval, if not parental benediction, and the only way to grab it was to throw your voice at him. It was speak or not be-noticed by my mother or my father so, quite frequently, we spoke our minds however mindless our response. But we believed in volume as a measure of our wisdom and we saw some strange connection between decibels and fact. The more loudly that we argued the more correct we thought we were.

My mother's dad was quiet though and my mother was like him. Unassuming and soft-spoken they were respected for their patience. So, when my mother's dad would join us at the table for his dinner, his tolerance for chaos was either slim or none-at-all. *"Basta tutti basta!"* is all he ever said and "enough!" is all he had to say and we completely understood. He was a solemn man with character and his actions were profound. So the fewer words that he would speak the more attentive we became.

He was christened 'John the Baptist' and he was truly apostolic. Giovanni di Battista Dabecco was his name. His creed was perseverance. His ethic was hard work. He taught by his example and we learned by what he did. He was slender, tall and striking with penetrating eyes and, when he was young, his wavy hair was thick and dark and full. He was firm but not too muscular and he could work an ox to death. He had the stamina of Moses and the endurance of a mule.

His father taught him how to work when he was just a boy. In Italy. Far south of Rome. In Corleto Perticara. It was a village near Potenza in the mountains of Lucania, where the stones were free and plentiful. Where he learned to chip and cut. Every church and home and local shop was hewn from *petra duro*. It was mined by hand and hauled by cart and sculpted into buildings. Some were marble. Some were fieldstone. Some were granite. Some were quartz. But all of it was quarried from the mountains, hills and valleys.

The inlaid roads were patterned in chromatic bands of color that were fitted and appointed with a decorative motif. Alternating cobbled stones of pink and yellow-amber led the people of his village to their chapels and their homes. Above the lintel of his doorway carved in elegant simplicity were the initials of his father on the house where he was born. These touches of humanity reflected who they were. They spoke of their devotion to the trade he would inherit.

I grew up in Pittsburgh where three rivers merge together. They birth a branch of the Ohio that becomes the Mississippi. It moves steadily and westward toward the farmland of this country and, ironically, my mother's dad would rather have lived there. He had come from rural Italy and he loved to turn the soil. He enjoyed the act of planting and the harvest he would reap. But instead he came to Pittsburgh, which was industrial and crowded, and the only plot of land he tilled was the yard behind his house. He dug it up and planted it. He seeded it and worked it. He grew every kind of vegetable that reminded him of home. He grew leeks and beets and fennel. *Radicchio* and *ciopolla*. *Ravanello* and *rapini* and *aglio* on the vine. He planted grapes to make his homemade wine and he grew eggplant and *zucchini*. He picked tomatoes by the bushel and he grew peaches, figs and pears. This was his passion. His obsession. His memory of home. It took him back to Perticara. To his village in the hills.

His garden was a respite from the rigors of his work, which was laborious, exhausting and difficult to find. In the midst of the depression when the economy was shattered – when people could not build a home and construction had been stopped – Giovanni worked on labor crews for pennies on the dollar. Roosevelt had funded the new WPA and he was one among the many who were conscripted in this way. For several years and many nights he would crawl on hands and knees. Laying down the streetcar tracks. The sidewalks and the curbs.

When the economy recovered, and he could practice his true craft, brick-by-brick and stone-by-stone he created where we lived. The communities and neighborhoods. The hospitals and homes. The schools and shops and theaters were built with his two hands. He gave more blood and sweat and tears to reinvent that place than did any politician who had ever taken credit. Like the men who came before him, and the trade that he had mastered, Giovanni was respected for his character and skill. Reflected in the toil of his grueling daily labor were the traditions and the legacy of Corletto Perticara.

I remember in his later years he would drive around the city. He would point to all 'his' buildings and 'his' streets and 'his' cathedrals. He spoke of them possessively because he built them all with pride. Quality and workmanship meant everything to him.

He was proud of every stone he carved and every brick he laid. He equated what he did in life with the man that he became. Many of those buildings still stand where they first stood and, nostalgically, I often dream that Giovanni is inside. I know without the slightest doubt that his spirit lingers on and I am humbled in the presence of 'his' pride-filled monuments. These are the relics that he left behind, for those who came to follow, like the workman in Corleto and the patterns in their streets.

Like the bricks that Giovanni stacked to fabricate each structure the daily meals my mother cooked provided our foundation. Every pinch of spice or sprig of herb was handed down to her. So in the making of our daily meals she sanctified our past. She resurrected and revived it. She honored who they were. Cooking was a legacy that paid tribute to her mother. It was an edible reminder of her family and her roots.

Our table was the meeting place for every generation. Not just for those descendants who would gather on that day. We were nourished by tradition and by the fruit of honest labor. We cherished what they did for us and who we had become. But more than nourish it sustained us. In our hearts and in our souls. It paid homage to the people who preserved our way of life.

The table was our Holy Land where grace and wisdom ruled. It was the source of all our knowledge from the time that we were born. It was our grade school and our high school and our college and our church. We gathered there as family to communicate and pray.

But dinner was the main event. An episodic *tour de force*. It was theater and drama. It was poetry in motion. We were merely actors on a very tiny stage and my father had produced us to be directed in this way. We talked about report cards and what happened in our lives. Or he reprimanded each of us for things we had not done.

But mostly we played silly games like Roller-Roller Ree. A simple game, but fun to play, and we played it all the time. The objective was to pick a 'thing'. A clock. A shirt. A bottle. Then give a clue or prompt or tip of what that thing might be. But the only hint that we could give was a letter not a word. Then each of us would prod and snoop by asking basic questions. And the answer to those questions would be either 'yes' or 'no'. "Is it blue?" Or "Is it round?" Or "Is it bigger than a breadbox?" If you identified the object then you controlled the game.

My father was the referee, the emcee and the host. Like a barker at a carnival he put the game in play. "Roller-Roller-Ree ... I see something that beginnns wiitthh ...G". He would drag it out, and roll his eyes, and pretend that he was thinking. But he knew what he was doing and he knew just what to say.

Although the object of our choosing was often quite obscure, it had to be within the room and visible, not hidden. At times we used psychology by choosing something simple. The more obvious the object the more difficult the guess. This went on for hours, until everyone was bored, then afterward we did our chores and mopped the kitchen floor.

My father had a standing rule that no one left the kitchen until the dishes and the pots and pans were washed and scrubbed and dried.

The floor was swept and lightly mopped and the garbage was removed. My father thought it only fair that we should clean the kitchen since my mother had prepared the meal that we had shoveled down. It didn't always work that way but we tried as best we could.

There was a master list of kitchen chores, and a matching list with names, and each of us were given a specific task to do. We even had rotations so that all the jobs were shared. So that no one scrubbed or mopped or schlepped more than once or twice a week. But even so it didn't work exactly as he planned.

The first job after dinner was to clear the kitchen table. To sponge it down and wipe it dry with soap and bleach and water. The last job was to mop the floor and to wax it once a week. Between the clearing of the table and mopping of the floor, the dishes and the pots and pans and the garbage were dispatched. If the game went on for hours, and the cleaning had to wait, then the person who was mopping would be stuck inside all night.

So we had a gentleman's agreement that allowed for changing shifts. If my brother Al was in hurry, and he couldn't wait to sweep, then he would switch with John or Paul who were assigned to clear the table. Then Al could be the first to leave but he would pull a double-shift. But even that was tenuous, because we always had an angle, and the more that we would change our shifts the more arguments ensued. So my father put his foot down, and put a stop to our arrangement, so that no one left the kitchen until all the jobs were done.

This routine was only broken on every other Thursday when the Bookmobile would make its rounds and open-up its stacks. It was always parked in Beechview near the trolley tracks at Broadway. Beneath the Pegasus of Mobil glowing brightly overhead. When the station closed in '64, and the Spic 'n Span moved in, the Bookmobile was forced to leave and find another spot. But even then it was important to have access to these books so my father put us in the car and drove us to the truck.

I remember the excitement that I felt when I was young. When at last I earned my reference card and the privilege to read books. I was eager and elated. I was zealous and inspired. I would grab as many hardback books as my skinny arms could carry and keep them for a week or two before exchanging them for others. It was the first time that I took control of the choices that I made and the choices that I did make were for science and for art.

The card that they had issued was my ticket to adulthood. It meant autonomy, maturity, independence and free choice. It was a license to be curious. I was a member of the club. My name was very neatly penned below the crest of William Pitt. Pitt's "Burgh" had then been given him by General John Forbes. He led a British expedition to capture Fort Duquesne. Beside the black and gold of William Pitt, which were the colors of his family, was an image of Carnegie who was synonymous with learning.

Above the door, and carved in stone, had been chiseled an inscription that changed the way the average man could learn from that time on. "Free to the People" read the message overhead. Freedom to be literate. Freedom to learned. Freedom to be equal to the educated man. It was an archive and a public trust that Carnegie had endowed so that anyone could learn to read and gain access to the world.

That was 1895, when it was founded formed and built, but by the time that I was ten years old Carnegie had gone mobile. The Carnegie card with coat of arms, and my name across the bottom, meant that I could borrow books and it wouldn't cost a cent. I kept that card for many years to remind me of that moment when I chose to learn more than I knew in ways that changed my life.

But the reason for this pilgrimage to the Bookmobile on Thursdays was that my father had encouraged us to read outside the classroom. In addition to our homework we were asked to read a story and to summarize what we had learned and to write a book report.

We could illustrate some principle, or make an oral presentation, and we were free to be inventive or creative or instinctive. But the intention was to demonstrate some basic understanding of the subject we had chosen and the meaning that it held. It didn't do us any good to read the Ten Commandments if we didn't truly comprehend the inherent connotations.

"Science for Beginners" was the first of many books where I learned to do experiments and to build things with my hands. I made an ant farm and a beehive and a functional volcano. I made a model of the human heart and a spaceship out of toothpicks. My father liked to build things too. And he built them very large. He built a totem pole with seven heads standing more than eight feet tall. He made plaster maps of Italy with grass and dirt and water. He built the Union ship, the Monitor, out of corrugated cardboard with turrets on a long flat deck with cannon balls and shells. It fought the southern ironclad Merrimac in 1862 and was the first of all known fighting ships to engage in civil war.

My father had instilled in us a very basic notion that the chances that you get in life depend on what you know. I had been a Cub Scout and a Webelo as a kid and the motto that they lived by was my father's motto too. Be prepared for anything and you will be just fine.

Even after dinner when we had finished all our chores. After the yelling and the screaming and the Roller-Roller-Ree. When our homework was completed and we had eaten and conversed. Still he offered something more to tweak our little brains.

Before we left the table, or the kitchen or the house, my father tried to tutor us. To open up our minds. He had visited a grade school, or the Board of Education, and bought some maps and globes and charts that were broken or discarded. He brought them home and made them new and hung them from the rafters. There was a family room adjacent to the kitchen near the table and he would line us up by age and size and sat is in a row. The chairs were placed each side-by-side along a seam in the linoleum and seated there we watched him and we listened as he taught.

We learned geography, topography, geology and planets. We memorized the Presidents and we knew where they were born. We learned mountain peaks and riverbeds and the deserts of the world. We learned the capital of every state and every foreign country. Mesmerized we sat there while my father asked us questions. Testing us on simple things that were mentioned twice before. But, no matter what the topic or the subject he would teach, he would use some map or prop or chart to emphasize his point. He would reach up to the rafter and he would pull and yank and tug. Then down a map of Africa or South America would come.

"Okay kids, geography." Or "Tonight we study Mars." Or "What would be the symbol for hydrogen peroxide?"

This was a logical extension of the table and the meal because it nourished both our bodies and our spongy little minds. The feeding of our stomachs and the seeding of our brains were equally important to my father at that time. He knew that growing fat and dumb was a useless combination. He would rather see us stout and smart. Or inquisitive and plump.

He nourished us consistently with food and information and we opened wide and swallowed almost everything he served. We would learn about the Orient and we would have a bite to eat. We would argue at the table just as easily as pray. We laughed and cried and pouted and we drank a little wine. But most of all we shared our love and celebrated life.

CHAPTER 3
WEEKENDS

Saturdays and Sundays have always been a joy. As a boy and as a skinny teen when I was younger than I am. When days were long and nights were slow and the future was a vision. When time was infinite and seamless and moved at it's own pace.

Saturday especially was the high point of the week. We had doughnuts in the morning with bacon, eggs and ham. The coffee perked and brewed and spit and filled the air with steam and the aroma of that coffee pot has lived with me years. I remember how it tasted from the first cup to the last. At five or six or seven or whatever time it was. My mother's brand was Eight O'Clock. Her mother brewed it too. The beans were whole and freshly ground and the pot was always full.

Scrambled by the dozen eggs were heaped into a pan. A heavy cast iron skillet that was old and black and burned. Years of family cooking had been scorched into that crock. The eggs went in with onion. Then potatoes. Then some cheese. Then freshly chopped tomatoes and some garlic and some salt. Then oregano and butter with paprika or Tabasco.

It was hot and it was spicy and we ate it by the pound. We made stacks of toast for breakfast by the piece and by the loaf. We would carve a hunk of fresh baked bread into twenty equal slices then line them up and grill them until crisp and golden brown.

The best toast that we ever ate was mother's homemade bread. It was fresh and firm and full and round and crusty and delicious. We didn't always toast it though. It was best straight from the oven. We would sneak it from the warming rack while it was hot and unattended and we would slice it down from end to end and smother it with butter. We smeared jelly, jam and marmalade or homemade fruit preserves. We sprinkled it with cinnamon or powdered it with sugar. When the bread was cut the steam would rise. The butter sizzled as it softened. We ate it fast and ate it hot and it melted in our mouth.

She baked her bread in volume. At least once or twice a week. Ten or twenty loaves of bread. Every shape and every size. Sesame and poppy seed and rustic and provincial. Tall and long or short and flat. Twisted rolled-and-tied. She stacked them on the counter in the corner near the furnace and covered them with linen and wrapped them in a sheet. Partially she did this to keep them fresh and moist but she also tried to hide them from our thieving little hands. She hid them in the blanket chest the closet or the dryer. Or she stored them in her bedroom and locked it with a key. But no matter where she hid that bread we found it and ate it.

The secret to the toast we made, besides my mother's homemade touch, was the toaster that had toasted all that bread for all those years. Extra wide and extra long the slots would hold the bread, then swallow it and crisp it up, and pop it out again. Up it sprung and out it shot like a bullet from a gun. Then load it up and press it down and shoot it out again. Down it went and up it came, through breakfast and through lunch, where assembly lines of hungry kids were pounding out that toast. The bread would fly the crumbs would fall and we would make a mess. But toasted, hot and buttered, nothing better passed our lips.

It took a constant daily beating that old toaster that we had. It wasn't new when I was young. It was on its second leg. It was a battered four-slice toaster that was salvaged by my father. He had found it in a restaurant or a diner that had closed. So home it came then on his bench he turned it upside down and, like Frankenstein and Igor, he tore its guts apart. New washers. New wiring. New handle.

New plug. A little soap and elbow grease and he made it new again. Completely fixed and functioning. Polished inside out. Ten years had passed since last its coils touched a piece of bread. But there it was, revived and clean, and ready for the toast.

This is what my father did when we were growing up. He would take an old and broken thing and repair it and reuse it. A radio. A table. A stereo. A lamp. He even found a car once. On a road not far from home. Abandoned in a shallow ditch and resting on its side. So he pulled it out and towed it home and propped it up on blocks. He fixed the brakes and tuned it up and made it run like new. He painted it and polished it and drove it for a year.

His hands I know were gifts from God. His father had them too. Whatever thing his hands would touch its life would be restored. But necessity, most certainly, was the reason for his craft. The need to make the best of things and to care for what we had.

So Saturday would start like this with coffee, toast and eggs. But the weekend promised something more than commotion and cuisine. The main event was yet to come and its coming was announced. Muffled voices. Clicking glasses. Laughter three floors down. It was the ritual beginning to the weekend and the fun. It was the Mardi Gras and Super Bowl all rolled-up into one. It was the calling of the faithful and it coaxed me from my bed. Down I'd come and round they sat. A table full of men.

The uncles gathered on this day to drink and smoke and swear. The table was their podium. It was their dais and their stage. Each would roast the other until each would have his turn. Their timing was impeccable. Their wit was sharp and sweet. And every joke I ever heard came first from those eight men.

They were the Keystone Cops and Chaplin. They were Abbott and Costello. They were Monty Hall and Groucho Marx and their nicknames that said it all. There was Jackass, Muzz and Hobey. Satacroach and Sarge. Ooge and Mr. Whispers. Fletcher Christian and the Cat. It was fantasy and fallacy and comedy and farce. I can't remember who said what, or who did what to whom, but I do remember laughing and I do remember them.

To think of them together still makes me laugh today. My dad would pour the whiskey and the boys would toss it back. The more they drank the more they talked and the more loudly they would laugh. Like moths around a campfire they were magnetic and inviting. They drew you in and held you. We listened and we grinned.

Much of what was said between the men around the table was either esoteric or blatantly risqué. They would laugh, so we would laugh, but we didn't have a clue.

At some point though, as time went on, we began to understand. And, as we caught-on to what they said, they caught-on to us. They heard us tell a joke or two that we had heard from them. Tawdry jokes and dirty puns. Words better left unsaid. At least by us, but not by them, they said them all the time. So, in order to prevent another breech of confidence, they disguised their conversations to protect us in a way. To keep us from repeating things that could embarrass or insult.

On the other hand, I realize now, that they were covering their asses. If our mothers ever heard their jokes repeated by a child, their days of bold impunity would have ended with a thud. No more jokes and no more beer and no more shots of whiskey. No more weekends with the uncles and no more stories to be told.

With banishment a certainty they devised a clever plan. They began to speak Italian. A dialect. A code. It was the language of their father from the town where he was born. A language from a southern town. From a village in the hills. A provincial town on winding slopes in the mountains by the sea.

And when they spoke this native tongue they acted out their parts. Their bodies spoke. Their gestures spoke. Their silence spoke as well. They would jump and twist and point and swat and pick and tweak and dance. And all of this had meaning in the language that they used. It was a supplemental grammar with exclamatory verve. It was an adjective or adverb used in rhythm or in rhyme. Their gestures and their cadence were inseparable for them. It was an orchestrated language. A choreography of words.

The laughter was insidious. Honest. Loud and pure. Hours past and stories flowed like honey from a jar. They did their shtick. They knew their parts. They did their imitations. Uncle Milty. Johnny Carson. Jessel, Burns and Allen. Laurel and Hardy. Amos and Andy. Abbot and Costello. A name came up and off they went. Solo or ensemble.

Their stories were incredible. Their imagery precise. They re-created memories as if time had never passed. They remembered everything in every last detail. Every gesture. Every nuance. Every word of dialog. It was a phantom apparition of a time-ago once lost. But their minds were keen and focused and they retrieved it with a thought. Photographic images appeared before our eyes. As tales were told and names recalled. As each revisited their lives. We never knew what they might say but we could not wait to hear them.

They loved it and they lived it and they invented their own fun. This I think came naturally. Their ability to speak. It was a way of life. A conscious act. A form of entertainment. Before video or television, radio was king. People listened when you spoke to them and they were honest with their feelings. They laughed and cried and comforted. They communicated well. Interaction was important and it was all that really mattered. So from early on they learned to share and to talk among themselves.

They told stories of adventure of survival and of hope. They reminisced about their childhood and their homeland and their parents. They fought the war but cherished peace and spoke of happiness and hardship. It was a way of life. Their way of life. And I loved to listen-in.

And, when the time had come each Saturday for one of them to leave, they would make some faulty lame excuse about the things they had to do. They would stand around and mumble. They would complain and bitch and moan. And time would pass and still they stood tugging at their pants. It was hard for them to separate because they loved to be together.

But when they left they left in style and they left the way they came. Cracking jokes and cursing and smoking bad cigars. The last thing that the men would do was to pour themselves a drink. To give a toast and toss one back to commemorate the day. The whiskey, like the toast they gave, remained the same for twenty years. Calvert was the brand they drank. Before Calvert was Carstairs.

My Uncle Felix was a salesman for both Calvert and Carstairs. So, naturally, the only booze that anyone would drink, was the whiskey that their brother sold from the basement of his house. The toast they gave was sacred so they didn't speak the words. They sang the words in harmony and they chanted and they droned. But first they had to clear their throats to warm their vocal chords.

"Hum..m..m. Hummmm..m..m..m..m. Hummmm..m..m..m..m."

And Felix, 'Mr. Punster', was the cantor for the chant. It was a somber chant but comic. It was Gregorian I think. It started low and deep and full as a monotonic hymn.

Felix posed like Mussolini standing stiff and stern and straight and he extended out his whiskey glass and he conducted with his drink. He would wave his hand and splash and drip as each one sang his part. They chanted and they chuckled and they bellowed out the toast.

"Rahm..m..m. Rahm..m..m..m. Rahm..m..m. Rahm-yah-nee-cuss. Pah-pan-yus. Tan-gyia-reen-us. Pohm..m..m. Pohm..m..m."

No one ever really knew what the hell it meant but no one ever really cared. It was just something that they did. They had fun with it. They played with it. They were all just kids at heart. They would click their glasses in the air. They said centanni or salute.

Then once again in unison their heads would all tip back. And down they poured their Calvert. And mockingly they'd shriek. "Yechhh", they'd say, "that's terrible. It's the worst I've ever tasted." They would grimace. They would make a face. They would pretend to spit it out. But Uncle Eugene made it very clear that they had an obligation. "It is up to us", he always said, "to drink this awful stuff. To keep it from the lushes and the harm that they might do."

Uncle Joe once spilled his whiskey, and the brothers were appalled, so he bent his skinny frame in half and he dropped down to his knees. He crouched as low as he could go and he licked it from the floor. He didn't really lick the floor he just acted out his part. They all cheered and each applauded. He smiled at them and winked. They laughed so hard, and shook and wept, that they nearly wet their pants.

As they left the house together they all huddled at the door. They thanked my mother for her kindness and they kissed her on the cheek. Then off they'd go to visit someone else along the way. To see another friend or two. To have another drink.

By now the time was ten o'clock, if barely ten at all, but on this day they made a point to visit every sibling. It was a tradition in our family. A way of keeping close. To remember where they came from. To remember who they were. It was a ritual necessity. It was a tribute to their parents. It was something never seen before. Nor have I seen it ever since.

But this was just the start of it. The beginning of the day. The rest of it seemed boring if not completely uneventful. The mundane came first. The cleaning. From the attic to the basement. We started in the bedrooms. On the third floor where we slept. Then we worked our way through every door and corridor and closet.

At one time there were four of us all sleeping in one room. Two squeaky beds with metal springs and a mattress that would droop. The closet space was limited but it didn't really matter. We would pile our grubby clothes in heaps between the dresser and the door. It drove my mother crazy, and it might have been untidy, but logically to our warped minds it was unbelievably efficient.

Early in the morning, when the uncles had departed, we were rounded up like lemmings and we were ushered to the kitchen. We were given strict instructions on how to clean the house and God forbid if we screwed up. We would never leave our rooms.

My father gave directions and distributed supplies. Rubber gloves and buckets. A scrub-brush and a mop. Brillo pads and sponges. A cleaning rag and soap.

When my father wasn't looking, or was digging in the garden, we tried to be inventive just to expedite our chores. We concocted chemicals and solvents in every combination, and we used them on the furniture, the carpet and the walls. We mixed Murphy's Soap and Comet with some Tidy Bowl and Pine-Sol. We decanted Lysol disinfectant into Mr. Clean and bleach. Once we mixed some Drano, which was an aerosol propellant, with some Bromide or peroxide, or some other kind of solvent. Then we flushed it down the toilet to clean the bowl and pipes. It fermented in the porcelain, and foamed and fizzed and frothed, then exploded like a time bomb and it blew the seat right off. We imploded all the plumbing from the third floor to the basement but, the objective was to clean the bowl, and we accomplished that quite well.

Top-to-bottom. Inside-out. We mopped and scrubbed and rinsed. And, as we did, my father watched. And we watched him right back. "Spotless" and "impeccable" were words he often used. When he said "clean", he did mean *clean*, with sweat and elbow grease. Sterilized and purified. Disinfected, washed and polished. Every inch of every room was subjected to this cleansing. To this sanitizing ritual. To this obsession that he had.

But still we tried to dodge this stuff with subterfuge and moxie. We conspired, cajoled and hedged our bets. We cut corners when we could. We did anything and everything to minimize our work.

He knew it though, and let it slide, but he never once forgot. And just when we convinced ourselves that he wasn't really watching, he would set us up and spring a trap and nail us to the wall.

On one occasion I recall he caught us in the act. We were told to wash the windows on both the inside and the outside. We were told to dust the lamp shades and to vacuum all the rugs. We had to strip the beds and wipe them down with some antiseptic solvent. We had to change the sheets and comforters then make the beds again.

But when we thought he wasn't looking we just skipped the 'cleaning' part. We fluffed the pillows and the mattresses and moved the furniture around. We opened all the windows to circulate the air. We pulled the sheers and closed the drapes to hide the film and dirt. We sprayed a scented disinfectant and hung some Airwick in the hallway so it smelled like we had scrubbed the walls even though we hadn't.

My dad came in and looked around and walked from room-to-room. He noticed that the beds were made and that the curtains had been drawn. He snooped and poked and lifted things and smiled and winked and joked. We were certain that we pulled it off so we asked if we could leave. Then he opened all the drapes and sheers. He turned on all the lights. He ran his fingers on the baseboard and the windowsills and doors. He checked for spider webs and dust balls in the corners of the bedroom. He stomped the carpet with his big black shoe to see if we had vacuumed. He even knelt beside the bed and ran his hand along the rail. The metal rail which held the slats that held the mattress and the box spring. Then he stood up straight and turned to me and I knew what he was thinking. I knew that look and what it meant. And I knew that we were busted. I stumbled back a foot or two and bumped into my brothers and they propped me up and waited for my father to explode. But to our relief he laughed at us and we nervously laughed-back. It was a game we played like hide-and-seek and this time we were found.

We knew why he would do these things. The dusting and the scrubbing. Self-sufficiency and discipline were important to my dad. He wanted us to realize how much effort that it took. To own a home. And keep a house. To be responsible and proud. There were ten of us that lived there. Thirteen from time-to-time. And when we got home the beds were made and the food was on the table. Our clothes were washed and folded and the house was always neat. But it didn't happen magically. My mother did that work. All by herself with little help and never was it easy. We learned by his example how rare my mother was and the point that he was making was that she was not our maid.

One day a week. Each Saturday. From ten o'clock to twelve. We washed and scrubbed and swept and cleaned and learned to love our mother.

But Saturday was more than this. More than Murphy's Soap and uncles. It was filled with things that mattered. At least they mattered to us then. With the uncles gone, and rooms well-groomed, we were free to carry on. To do those things that all kids do when there is nothing else to do. Thinking back its curious the things that I remember. The moments that have meaning now are those memories of home. Not friends or kids or outdoor games or theaters or baseball. Not girlfriends or dances or field trips or high school. Not Cub Scouts or Boy Scouts or Webelos or Eagles. It was the time I spent with family. With my brothers and my sister. With my mother and my father and my uncles and my cousins. Family life was everything and nothing interfered.

On Saturday or Sunday, on those summer afternoons, we would cook out on the patio and play *bocce* in the yard. My dad would throw some sausage or some burgers on the grill and make *caprese insalata* with tomatoes from our garden. With homemade mozzarella. Creamy, soft and moist. With freshly picked oregano. Or rosemary. Or basil. We would crack it with the pepper and sprinkle it with salt. Then extra virgin olive oil drizzled over top. The bread was warm. The wine was chilled. We ate and played and talked.

The Italian game of bocce is equivalent to bowling, except the game is played outdoors, on lawns or courts of clay. It's a simple game with balls, not pins, and the objective is to argue. Two teams of giocatore, with four players on each side, have a palla or pallone, which is a very heavy ball. The pallina is the object ball and it's smaller than the others. The giocatore throws the palla and aims for the pallina. And the closer these two balls converge the giocatore wins the point. Unless of course we challenged. And we challenged every time. Every micro-macro-millimeter was judiciously confirmed and we did this with a twig or stick or a piece of broken string.

Anything that we could find to measure every toss was used to challenge and interpret and to argue every point. It was CSI for bocce. It was forensic evidence. We questioned one's paternity, or one's failing, faulty eyesight. We challenged one's virility, veracity and virtue. But, that's the way the game was played, and that's the way we liked it.

If the weather were too cold or wet for bocce and a cookout then quickly we would improvise and move it all inside. My dad would drag the table from the kitchen to the game room and we would have our picnic in the basement of the house.

CHAPTER 3

My mother made our favorite food no matter what the combination
and we ate it at the table while we watched our favorite shows. She
made meat balls and hot dogs and coleslaw and pizza. *Pasta e fagioli*
and Jell-O and soup. We drank root beer from the bottle and freshly
brewed iced tea. Or lemonade. Or Kool-Aid. Or some frozen green
concoction.

We watched matinees and westerns or comedies and dramas.
Our heroes were adventurous, audacious and courageous. From
Robin Hood and Zorro to Robinson Crusoe. We imitated Hercules.
We pretended to be Sampson. We sailed with Jason and the
Argonauts and cheered for Spartacus. We flew with Sky King in the
Song Bird and laughed at Mr. Ed. We idolized the Bowery Boys and
fought the Dead End Kids.

Our favorite though was Tarzan and we couldn't get enough. We
knew every episode and story line. Every twist and turn and plot. We
knew the actors and the elephants and the lions all by name. We
knew where to find Palmyra and the secret Tarzan yell. We knew
Simba from Ungowa and the good chiefs from the bad. And we memorized the titles of every single show. *Tarzan the Ape Man. Tarzan and
his Mate. Tarzan Escapes. Tarzan Finds a Son. Tarzan's Secret Treasure. Tarzan's New York Adventure.*

The best of all the Tarzan shows that ever were produced featured
Johnny Weissmuller and the great Maureen O'Sullivan. Johnny
Sheffield played the little Boy and Cheetah was the chimp. Johnny
had that certain look. He was convincing as a savage. Maureen and
John, as Jane and Boy, had a chemistry that worked.

Together they were magic and they brought Africa to life and they
made it seem so plausible to live among the apes.

It was the same thing in the evenings when we sat around the
Philco. Or it could have been a Zenith. Or DuMont. Or Motorola.
With cathode tubes in black-and-white and rabbit-ear antennas. We

were used to shades-of-grey until 1961. With oscillating wavelengths and racks of vacuum tubes. Fluorescent beams of dappled light and synchronizing signals. Then RCA and Disney conspired to change the airwaves with monochrome contraptions and the Wonderful World of Color.

We liked to watch Walt Disney and to hear that cricket sing. The animation was amazing and the stories were inspiring. Toby Tyler was my favorite but I liked to watch them all. My mother loved Ed Sullivan for the variety and music. For the spinning plates and acrobats and the dancers with batons. Topo Gigio was a regular. Senior Wences was an icon. He introduced the Beatles, Barbara Streisand and The King.

My dad preferred the nature shows like Safari and Wild Kingdom and all of us looked forward to Mitch Miller and his band. He would end his show with sing-a-longs so we sang-along with Mitch. The bouncing ball would jump and leap and follow every word. And we would read and bounce and sing and follow right along. We did these things together as a family and as friends. So for many years I did not know that friends were not related.

Sunday was the same for us. There was a certain ebb and flow. It was predictable in many ways but never quite the same. In the morning we would go to the church for Catechism lessons. Then after class we went to Mass from twelve o'clock to one. After Mass we stopped for coffee in the parish social hall. After that we had our dinner. Then everyone went home. After dinner we watched Disney. Then Sullivan. Then bed.

We always had our dinner in the early afternoon. So that everyone could visit but still be home by dusk. Sunday was supposedly for rest and contemplation. But the cooking and the visiting were less restful than exhausting.

Sisters and mothers and brothers and cousins. Nieces and nephews and in-laws and aunts. It was chaotic, not relaxing, on these Sabbath afternoons, and there was nothing more to contemplate than where to find a seat. People came from everywhere. Often more than I could count. It took years to learn the names of all those relatives and cousins. It was hard for me to memorize who belonged to whom. Some had not been relatives just friends-of-friends-of-friends. Some of them came once or twice and were never seen again. Some of them would never leave no matter how we tried.

The weekend was communal in a way which was profound. In our Church and in my parent's home. At the altar and the table. It was a metaphor. A way of life. It was the core of who we were. It was a time for us to celebrate and to be one among ourselves.

WEEKENDS

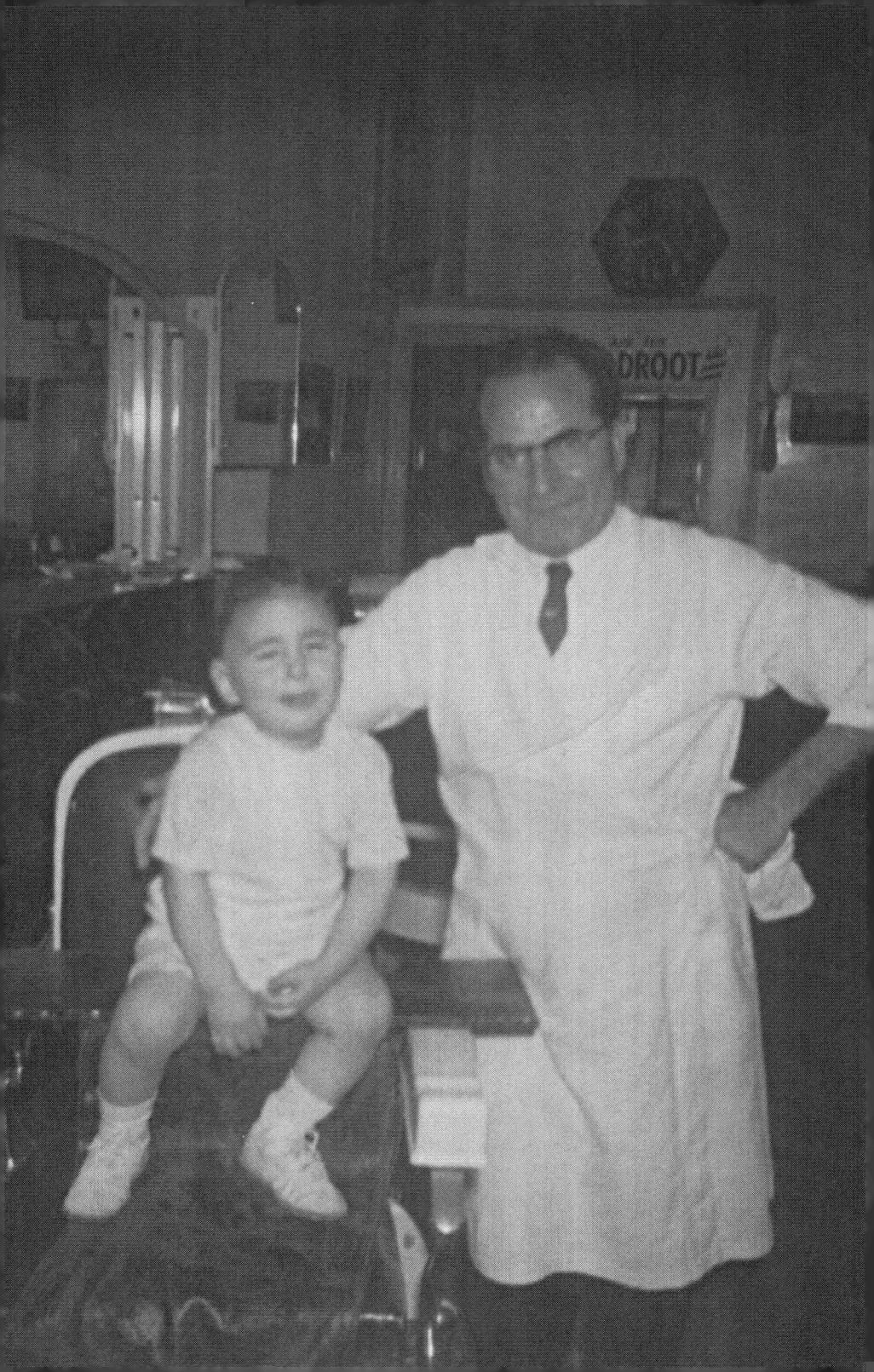

CHAPTER 4
TONY THE BARBER

His real name wasn't Tony. It was Benito De Silvestri. But 'Benito' didn't seem to fit so instead he went by 'Tony'.

"A barber should be Tony not Benny or Benito. Benito is my given name, but in the trade I'm known as Tony."

He used that name for sixty years. An alter ego as it were. An a.k.a. A nom de plume. An alias assumed. And the man we knew as Tony was a man to reckon with.

Tony loved to take his evening walks. It was a custom that he cherished. It was a habit that he carried from his village in the mountains. The *passeggiata* was the nightly stroll in the courtyard or piazza. It was a promenade. A saunter. It was a social affectation. Unmarried and available the men would strut-their-stuff as the women watched from windows or from the balconies above. Young men dressed in suits and ties, or the finest clothes they owned, walked slowly and deliberately intending to be seen. The evening walk was playful. It was civilized and friendly. It was a form of daily exercise in a very public setting.

And this is just what Tony did every evening after dinner. A mile or two up Broadway to Potomac Avenue then back again to Wenzell by the trolley tracks at Neld. Then Broadway to his barbershop near Coast and Hampshire Streets. He kept that pace for many years and he never missed a day. He would stop and talk with friends of his or he would wave as he passed by. On occasion he would slow his pace a block or two from home and share a glass of homemade wine with his expatriate companions. But mostly he just walked his walk as smartly as he dressed. He stood behind his chair all day so this would help him to relax.

But people change and places change and our neighborhood changed too. Strangers came and families went and friendships always suffered. It affected how we lived our lives when that transformation came. Our traditions and our habits so familiar to us then were altered if not ended and it was difficult to bear.

One night Tony walked his walk from Broadway to Potomac. He went south along the boulevard past the monument at Shiras. That monument was placed there in 1940-something to recognize the soldiers who had fought in World War II. It was a solid pier of cast concrete, with an eagle at the apex, and on each side were lists of names which identified each man. The plaques were bronzed and polished and the soldiers were arranged with last name first, and first name last, but no mention of their rank. It was the sacrifice that each had made, not the rank each may have held, that shown the spirit of the monument and the honor it bestowed.

My father's name is on that plaque with his brothers and his friends. My uncles lived. My father lived. But many friends did not. It was a monument to valor, and to those who served our country, but on the night that Tony passed it was commandeered by vandals.

As he walked that night along the street past the monument near Brusco's he was threatened and insulted and confronted and cajoled. Some bonehead kid from Alton Street who could barely spell his name wanted some excitement and Tony was his mark. So he barked at him and picked a fight and he tried to scare him off but Tony stood his ground that night and commanded their respect.

"For years", he said in heavy tones of broken English-cum-Italian, "for years I walk these streets alone and nobody never stops me. I don't stop now unless I want. I don't stop now for you."

He walked away and headed home. They laughed and cursed and spit. But Tony wasn't gone for long. He was back by ten o'clock. He was diminutive but forceful. They were big and loud and crude. He defied them and confronted them and he wouldn't back away. He picked the biggest oaf and loudest mouth and the strongest in the group. Then he reached inside his pocket. Pulled his gun and cocked the hammer. He pointed it and shook it. He told them what to do with their childish pranks and idle threats and their insults and their jokes. And if anyone was brave enough they could try to take him down. But if they did he made it clear that someone would bet hurt.

"If you touch me. If you harm me. If you do anything to me. One of you will die before you finish what you do."

He looked at every one of them and stared them in the eye. And as calmly as a Buddhist Monk he tipped his hat goodbye.

Tony walked those streets alone at night – most every night until he died – and no one ever touched him nor dared to say a word.

Now this is quite a story had just anyone done this but Benny, known as Tony, was eighty-one years old. With self-respect and nerves of steel, and a broken empty gun, Tony kept his dignity and never even flinched.

Tony was our barber. The only one we knew. He gave me my first hair cut when I was barely two years old. I was squirming. He was smirking. My father snapped the shot. And all around my head and feet were curly locks of hair. Soft and fine and long and brown. My identity since my birth. My mother cried. I know I cried. But Tony was amused. My mother kept those locks of hair, in her cedar chest at home, in a clear waxed paper envelope with that photograph of me.

I was not the only kid to sit before the master. Everyone I ever knew had to face him through the years. Sooner, if not later, and at some point down the road, you found yourself in Tony's chair. There was no place else to go.

That chair of his was big and green with genuine faux-leather. It was cold and clean and washable and it swiveled as it spun. It pumped and moved and lurched and leaned. It moved forward. It moved backward. It moved up and down and front-to-back and he controlled it with his foot. It had a pedal with an ornate grille that protruded from the base and he played it like an organ in the holiest of churches.

Placed upon this green hydraulic dragon that you rode, a safety belt would cinch you tight, until you couldn't move a finger. Head-to-toe and side-to-side, firmly you were fastened, to dissuade the slightest movement and the damage it might cause.

Tony smiled and raised an eyebrow. Then you held your breath and prayed. Once your butt was buckled-in Tony owned your soul.

Tony was a surgeon not a barber with his tools. He wore a long silk tie and clean white shirt that was stiff and starched and collared. With pleated trousers, creased and striped. With cuffs and hidden pockets. Suspenders held his pants in place which came to rest against his shoes. Buffed and polished. Black and pointed. Laced and firmly tied. Judging by his wardrobe he should have sat behind a desk with pipe in hand and leather chair and a three-piece tailored suit.

But even so the clothes he wore were hidden by a smock. A clean white linen overcoat protected his attire. It was a stylish tunic jacket that buttoned at the side. Like a dentist or a doctor. He looked dapper and refined. He wore gold bifocal glasses that reflected in the light. And a pinky ring and cuff links. And a stickpin in his tie. Not the image of a small town clip who cut the neighbors' hair. He looked more like Salk or Einstein. Fleming or Marconi. He was impeccable. Meticulous. Articulate. Exact.

The shop as well was surgical. Green and squeaky clean. Sterile and immaculate. Odiferous. Pristine. In later years he came to grow a pencil thin mustache. Slightly curved and debonair. It was stylish and unique. He thought himself an artist or artistic to be sure. The evidence was everywhere of his secret avocation.

On the wall above the hard wood chairs, on the chairs we sat to wait, hung a painting of his garden and the yard behind his shop. Precise and geometric. He envisioned what he drew. He had transformed the vegetation into topiary art. The designs he made on paper for the plants and trees and grass were brought to life by seed and soil and shaped by his own hands. The painting of the yard behind his shop, which was his house, was faithful to the vision that he had captured in his art. Roses and vineyards and birdbaths and bushes. Hedges and flowers and lanterns and trees.

More than able, he was masterful, with scissors and a comb. He was an artist and an artisan. He was Picasso and Pasteur. The scissors were his scalpel and the comb was like a chisel. He could sculpt a head of frizzy hair into a classic Roman bust.

On the other hand he couldn't smell. He had no sense of his own senses. So he always showed a penchant for toiletries that stank. He used greasy creams and bad colognes that he anointed like a cleric. He would scoop some awful scented goop and rub it on your hair then slick it back and comb it and paste it to your head.

Wildroot. Brillcream. Vaseline or kerosene. These all smelled the same to him so he didn't really care. I must have been combustible when I finally left his shop and the remnants of that wretched stuff is still embedded in my scalp. I think of him each time I shave or buy a tank of gas.

He used strips of scented tissue, white and long and thin, that he wrapped around my skinny neck and pinned tightly with a clasp. It was a simple way to catch the hair as it fell below the collar but it choked and scratched and burned and itched. It was more annoying than convenient. Then he covered me from neck-to-knees with a long black silky bib and, against the whiteness of the tissue-strip, I was transformed into a priest. Then he showered me with talcum when he finished with my head and I sat there in a cloud of dust like Charlie Brown or Linus.

Those tonsorial accouterments were important to the man. The swivel chair and bad cologne. The spectacles he wore. The talcum and the powder and the paper and the comb. The scissors and the mirrors and the painting of his garden.

Tony was methodical in everything he did. Evangelical. Maniacal. Committed to his craft. It was a spiritual awakening to sit in that man's chair. We were a sacrificial offering and Tony held the knife.

The most unnerving day with Tony came when I was nearing adolescence. Sometime after puberty but before I hit fifteen. My hair was thick and heavy and I had whiskers on my chin and my sideburns and my mustache had just begun to grow. These were the signs of coming manhood for a post-pubescent boy and a certain rite of passage was required to mark this day. Tony knew instinctively that it was time to use 'the knife'. A cold hard blade of sharpened steel. A razor with a handle. He would raise his arms and twist his wrist and rotate with each stroke. He would place it on my tender skin and pull and tug and flick. He scraped the fuzz around my bulbous ears and below my Roman nose. He deftly cropped my un-cleft chin with dexterity and grace. And with a final flip of flashing steel I transcended adolescence. I had been ushered into manhood. I had been given my first shave.

Tony had a leather strop that hung beside his chair and he used it like a grindstone to sharpen all his blades. The leather had been chipped and sliced from years of daily use. Three inches wide and one inch deep. It was a fixture in his shop. The blade he used that fateful day was long and thin and sharp. It was hidden in the handle of a pearl-white inlaid case. He used that blade for many years. He brought it with him on the boat. And it fit his hand as naturally as a finger or a thumb. It was a symbol of his station. His profession and his life.

Quickly, but quite casually, he flipped the blade until it clicked. Then he slapped the strop repeatedly in syncopated time. I got lost in all the rhythm of the steel against the leather. He played it like an instrument and it was soothing to my ears. But when he was done, and it was sharp, he would brush it on his skin. He moved the blade along his arm to see if it would snag. And if it did he cursed out-loud then sharpened it some more. He would hold it up and turn it toward the light behind the chair and it reflected like a crystal fob or the facets of a diamond. He could tell if it was sharp or dull by the way the light refracted. His eye was like a microscope and he detected every flaw.

With this final test of sharpness, and with laser-like inspection, he would touch my head and bend it. Very gently. Very slowly. With his thumb and with his finger he would control my every movement. Like a gyroscope in outer space my head would twist and float. He would turn my head and bend it until my chin was in my chest.

He owned some chrome and glass contraption that was electrically supplied that took shaving cream and heated it and pushed it through a coil. And from the coil to the nozzle that was used to heat the foam he would press a simple lever and it would froth into his hand. He would scoop it out with one hand and he would smear it with the other. Then he would trace around my face and ears. Then across my neck and chin. Every inch of every pore was lathered with this cream. *Non si muova*, he would say, "Do not move, Signore Raimondo." I would tense and groan and pray. He would laugh and shake his head.

Of course he couldn't hear me because my heart was in my throat. Caruso played and Tony sang and he conducted with his blade. Foam would fly with every note or with each gesture that he made like Antonio Vivaldi wielding a baton. I sat frozen in that cold green chair, sweating as I prayed, and I counted every minute with each movement of his blade. I felt it pull and tug and pluck and scrape across my skin. And with every stroke he stopped or paused to wipe-away the foam. On my shoulder. On his tunic. On a towel or on the chair. He would clean the blade and take a breath then hum another tune. He sang as he conducted with my face still in my shirt. Then the tonic and the talcum and the grease and cheap cologne.

And when it stopped it stopped completely. The singing and conducting and the cutting and the grease. He pressed the pedal or the lever and the chair would hit the floor and he spun me toward the mirror and he crossed his arms and stared. I turned to face the brightness of the lights against the mirror and I squinted and I focused and I tried to shield my eyes. The first thing was to check my ears, making certain they were there, and after that I didn't care I was happy to be free.

He was fast, I grant him that but, for minutes that seemed hours, my contorted face and twisted neck were held against their will. If I tried to move the slightest bit, to sneeze or gasp for air, his fingers on my lathered neck would tighten like a vise.

He would hold my head and bend it until my breathing was impaired and he warned me of the consequence if I tried to move again. I knew that he was just concerned. If I moved I might get cut. But, in my early teens and cowardly, it scared me half to death.

He peeled the wrap around my neck and removed my priestly garb. He dusted it and flicked it and he snapped and it popped. He draped it on his forearm and took me by the hand and as he helped me from the big green chair. He said *Grazie, Signore*. I paid the man. I shook his hand. Then I ran right out the door.

Tony always called me 'Mister'. *Signore* in Italian. Even as a little kid he would address me with respect. He was respected and respectful, and I trusted him for that, so in return he trusted me and the circle was unbroken. I never thought of Tony as a barber after all. He was businessman. Professional. Even corporate in a way. To our family he was Benny. He was the man behind the smock. 'Tony' was a figment of our friend's imagination but 'Benny' was the family friend who shared his life with us. He cared for us. We cared for him. We cared for one another.

I told him once that painting was a passion in life. I told him as I sat there in that green iconic chair. I would talk and he would cut and we would have this conversation. I would tell him that I liked to draw and that writing wasn't easy. That I liked to read the classics. That I was interested in art. I told him that I played guitar and that I tried the clarinet. That music and the opera had inspired me to create.

When I mentioned these obsessions Tony seemed a bit surprised and without another word from him he put his comb aside. He told the two men in the waiting room to see him after lunch. Then he closed the shop and pulled the blinds and locked the door behind them. He whisked me off abruptly as he yanked me from the chair with the apron on my shoulders and lather on my face. He led me to a narrow door near the corner of his shop then he opened it and dragged me in before I ever knew what happened.

It was a simple door. A wooden door. With paneled glass and paint. It had no lock or bolt or latch but it might as well be steel. It protected his identity. His privacy. His heart. It separated what he did from who he was in life. Tony here and Benny there. The barber and the man. It divided not connected the two worlds in which he lived and that four-inch door of wood and glass was as symbolic as his razor.

For a child my age, as I was then, it was a journey far away. It was adventure and discovery. I was exploring the unknown. From his chair and through that door that led into his home took twenty steps or maybe more. Less I think not more.

Then suddenly and mystically a room appeared like magic and in this room hung sketches of the Ancient Roman Forum. There were drawings of the Seven Hills and the Arch of Constantine. There was a print by Veronese and a chalice by Cellini. Each of which were replicated perfectly from photos. There was a model of the Pantheon and the Baptistery in Florence and there were paintings of Nicastro and pastels of Catanzaro. Some were framed or trimmed in wood. Some were covered under glass. Some were wrapped in plastic. All shielded and protected from the dust and talc and hair.

I was mesmerized and dazzled. Astonished and surprised. By the quantity and quality of everything he had. Some of it he painted and some of it he bought. Some of it he carried from his homeland years before. They were a tangible reminder of the life he once abandoned but Italy was everywhere behind that four-inch door.

He shared his views and shared his thoughts and he asked for my opinions. He quoted men of letters and he knew the Masters well. I saw him not as Tony but the man behind the door. He was Benito De Silvestri or just Benny to his friends.

There were times I sat outside that door at noon or just past one waiting for a haircut while he was having lunch inside. I could see him as a silhouette. An apparition through the blinds. I could hear him on the telephone or speaking with his wife. I could smell the food right through the door and I could picture what he ate.

On the day of that first visit, with the lather and the apron, he asked if I would join him at his table for a meal. But on that day I could not wait although I can't remember why. School I think. Or homework. But I didn't want to leave. It was the first time ever in my life that I was treated as an equal. As intelligent and capable. I was valued for my thoughts.

The food was rich and wonderful and it reminded me of home. The sauce simmered in a cast iron pot and there was pasta on the stove. He had homemade bread and dandelions and decanters filled with wine. He had *parmigiana* and *prosciutto* hanging in his kitchen and I could taste the ravioli and the pesto with my eyes. The pots and pans and cans and spoons were the same that mother used and the aroma from that pantry was enough to make me fat.

My family is from Italy, like Benny and his wife, from the province and the county near the village where they lived. In the ankle of the mountains only minutes from the sea with the Tyrrhenian on one side and the Ionian the other. So much of what his wife had cooked our family cooked as well. They brought it from the countryside to the cities where they settled.

Benny and Pasquale were friends in their hometown. It was a southern town in Italy where each had learned their craft. Nicastro was a village, or at least it was back then, where Benny learned to barber and Pasquale tailored clothes. Pasquale was my father's dad. He was my nonno in Italian. And *'compare'* was the word they used when they would speak among themselves. It meant 'companion' or 'compatriot'. It signified respect. It was an honor to be chosen to be one among these men. It was a sign of admiration and of friendship and of age. It was reserved for just the fewest and the dearest of old friends. Pasquale Vennare. Nicola Pellegrino. Giovanni Dabecco. Benito De Silvestri – *amici tutte*.

All of them were humble men. And gentle men. And strong. A tailor and a barber and a mason who cut stone. They suffered for their labors and their craft that few still know. Their livelihoods, and very lives, depended on their hands. Aging hands and wrinkled hands that were failing through the years. But tenacious hands and nimble. Experienced but frail.

CHAPTER 4

Benny and Pasquale had been friends for many years. They had
met in Catanzaro when both were very young. They made a vow when
they were living in that *villagio Montagnoso*. When they were strong
and proud and fit. Before they moved away. They decided that their
friendship would last throughout their lives. That, no matter what no
matter where, they would always be together.

More than that, he told me, was the vow of *sepoltura*. They committed to each other to be together when they died. Whoever first
would pass away between these two best friends the other, who survived his death, would lead him to the grave. It was a pact between
two lifelong friends made many years ago in a village on a long dirt
road in Provenza Catanzaro.

Benny told me of the sepoltura many years ago. It stunned me
then and it shakes me now to think of that devotion. A bond between
two loving men and the respect that both had shared that lasted
almost eighty years until Pasquale passed away. And true to his com-
mitment Benny honored his old friend. He told my aunt about their
sacred vow made many years ago and the pledge that both had given
to be present in the end. That time was now. The place was here.
And he was not to be denied.

But Angeline the matriarch had made some other plans. The children of his children were to bear his casket now. From the parlor to
the family church. From the altar on to the grave. But Pasquale's
friend would not let go and he made it very clear. I gave my word. We
took an oath. I promised my old friend.

So as an honorary bearer Benny took his place in line. On the
shoulders of his children's sons rode Pasquale on that day but out in
front stood Benny as he led them to the grave.

Solemnly he walked before the casket of Pasquale and cried the
tears of friendship that ended on that day. He simply said "good-bye
my friend" then slowly walked away.

An era passed. A lifetime passed. But Benny kept his word. I saw that day a loyalty that I may never see again. A sense of love and obligation. Of fidelity and pride. A simple code of honor that went with them to their graves.

Pasquale was the first to go. Then Benny's wife would die. Cancer took her slowly as he suffered by her side. The pain was his as well as hers and it drained him of his fight. Then he died too within a year from cancer like his wife. But Benny did not leave this world like Pasquale or his wife. He stayed at home and died in bed behind that four-inch door.

CHAPTER 5
DICK THE HANDY MAN

I never knew his last name but we always called him Dick. He was here and there and everywhere at any given time. He was a kindly man. But quiet. He was alone for many years. He was a handyman. A laborer. A gardener. A mason. His back and arms and legs and sweat were his only tools in trade.

His life was sad and troubled. Or it seemed that way to me. His wife had long since passed away but he still suffered at her loss. The neighbors gave him food and soap. The priest supplied his clothes. And everything he ever owned was carried in a bag. It was a satchel cut from burlap sacks that were used for shipping onions. He pulled them from a garbage heap and he shaped handles out of wire.

His canvas pants were sewn and stitched. They were crudely patched and mended. A twisted braid of salvaged rope held his trousers to his hips. He would wrap the cord around his waist and tie it in a knot. His boots were ragged. Scuffed and tattered. They turned upward at the toe. The heel on one had worn away and the soles were paper thin.

He wore a faded shirt. A fitted vest. A narrow threadbare tie. And never would he show himself without dressing in a coat. I have always been in awe of him. The pride he must have felt. He was a simple man who scratched the dirt. Deprived of daily comforts. But still had the dignity to wear a shirt and tie.

His flannel vest was thinly striped. It was brushed and dark and flat. His shirt beneath his waistcoat was buttoned to the neck. Tightly buttoned. Firmly clasped. The collar pinched his skin. He

CHAPTER 5

worked like that. In shirt and tie. In any kind of weather. Hauling refuse in the winter. Digging tree stumps in the rain. Still he wore his uniform. His shirt and vest and tie.

On short grey hair was placed a cap. A simple black beret. It was angled on his forehead and it drooped above his brow. Not rakishly but casually. As if it seemed by chance. Too large perhaps for his small head but he wore it nonetheless. It was stretched and worn and stained and frayed from years of sweat and pain. From every season in the elements or the dampness of his skin.

He lived impoverished but grateful in the basement of a building, which had been many things for many years, from a dance hall to a church. Built by Harrah as a movie house, in the twenties or the thirties, the Legionnaires would bivouac through the forties and the fifties. It was a pool hall and a bowling lane until 1985 when it converted to a rest home for the poor and underprivileged. Ironic after all these years that such a fate befell this building. Dick himself should be the one to occupy that place.

He walked the streets and alleys with his bundle at his side. He knocked on doors and begged for work that no one else would touch. Menial. Laborious. Exhausting and relentless. He toiled and he tussled and he struggled with the earth. He dug trenches in the winter when the ground was frozen solid. He carried cinder blocks and slag stone and he mixed mortar with a hoe. He chopped fodder into compost. He hauled garbage on his back. This was his life. This was his fate. This was the only thing he knew. He was serene and he was tranquil when he was working with his hands.

One summer day when I was ten or maybe in my teens I recall an episode that has stayed with me for years. I was walking to the bakery. To Patty Cake or Kribble's. From Fallowfield to Broadway past Serano's Hardware store. I crossed the trolley tracks to Hampshire at the corner next to Islay's. I was walking down the sidewalk toward

62

the Alpine Bar and Lounge. It was hot and it was humid. It was an arid summer day. I hadn't seen the handyman for days or weeks or months.

In the middle of the sidewalk in the middle of the day I came upon the handyman motionless and bent. Some would pass as if he wasn't there. Others pointed, laughed or stared. Some mumbled foul obscenities and brusquely stepped aside. He was oblivious to all of this. The taunting and the jeers. He was distant and expressionless as I hurried to his side.

But just as I approached the man to help him to his feet the chiming of the church bells broke the stillness of the moment. They pierced the staleness and the dryness of that tepid afternoon. They rang loudly. They rang sharply. They rang steadily and brightly. They rang each day. Three times a day. At twelve and three and six.

It was the Angelus. The daily prayer. To commemorate the dead. It was a ritual tradition. An acknowledgement of Life. The Incarnation of the Faithful. An incantation for the soul. When the bells announced the Angelus the faithful would abide and as devoutly as a man could pray Dick was on his knees.

In reality the Angelus was difficult to practice. Not seven hundred years ago but in 1963. The origin of Angelus was a calling to the pagans. The bells would prompt the farmers and the peasants in the field to pause and rest and contemplate the power of redemption. To reject their heathen Godless past. To acknowledge their new Faith. The morning bell commemorates the Resurrection from the tomb. At noon the bell acknowledges the Passion of the Christ. The hours and the moments before his crucifixion. The evening bell epitomized the Incarnation of the flesh. When after death and resurrection came the Heavenly descent. The Word made flesh. The promise kept. The redemption we all seek.

CHAPTER 5

Francois Millet once lionized this humble prayerful theme. Monumental and Immutable. Iconic. Archetypal. A man and women in the field. A peasant and his wife. Hat in hand and bent in prayer with a pitchfork and a basket. Meditating mendicants digging for potatoes. A plea for those less fortunate. For the poor departed souls.

The Angelus had meaning then. It was encouraged by the Church. It was embedded in the psyches of the faithful and the pious. It was a daily proclamation born of solace and compassion. An act of pure devotion and fidelity and faith. That image of the Angelus once painted by Millet was copied and collected more than any work of art. It was an unpretentious image of humility and grace. A symbolic affirmation of the Sermon on the Mount. Righteous are the humble and blessed are the meek.

What stays with me these many years were those cold and callous comments. Those sharp and slashing hateful stares that cut him like a knife. I saw that day hypocrisy and prejudice and rancor before I even understood the meaning of those words. The only one among them truly worthy of respect was on his knees and praying for the salvation of their souls. For his gentility and prayerfulness he was derided and disparaged yet never did he raise his voice nor react in any way.

Dick would help my father. On occasion. Now and then. And my father helped the handyman as often as he could. He was Italian. Calabrese. He was one among the many. He could have been an uncle or a cousin or a friend. He had the features and the accent that were common to our culture. He was an immigrant. A laborer. A *compaesano* just like us. We saw in him a refugee more destitute than others and we knew that only circumstance had saved us from his fate. He was more than just a handyman. He was determined, proud and honest. He was rugged and dependable. He had integrity and heart. It was a function of his character. He took pride in what he did. It was the core of who he really was and we identified with that.

One afternoon in August, the handyman arrived, with pick in-hand and burlap sack. In shirt and vest and tie. He was hired to prune some shrubs and trees. To tidy-up the yard. He had to move the Rose of Sharon from the wall behind the kitchen and plant them near the patio at the boundary of our yard. My Uncle Felix lived on one side and we lived on the other and the massive Rose of Sharon formed a wall of living color.

I watched him dig those bushes as he coaxed them from the soil. He would handle them as gently as an infant in a crib. I know that they were heavy but he moved with grace and ease. Everything seemed effortless. It was natural for him. He took his time and bound the roots. He wrapped the branches and the leaves. Then one by one he scooped them up and carried them away. He dug each hole quite carefully with symmetrical precision. Each pit was sharp and deep and round. They fit perfectly inside. He did this all by intuition. He took no measurements or readings. He was attentive and perceptive. He was clairvoyant with a spade.

When he had finished potting every tree, every shrub and bush and flower, he would brush them with his fingers and he would water each by hand. He didn't use a garden hose. He used a bucket and his hands. He drew the water from the spigot into a pail that he would carry. It was old and it was dented. It was galvanized but rusted. He would tie it to the belt loop of his tattered canvas pants. It was his calling card. His doorbell. It would clang as he would walk. He would cup his hands and dip them in then lift them out again. Then tenderly and lovingly he would sprinkle every shrub. He nurtured them and pampered them. He cradled and he rocked them. He reminded me of Kreskin. He was uncanny in this way. There was a sense of psychic energy between his hands and what he touched.

There was an irony in this old man who was impoverished and homeless. Caring for a blade of grass more than others cared for him. I was moved to see my father put his arms around this man.

With friendship and compassion. With admiration and respect. Dick was genuine. Benevolent. He was respectful if not child-like. I felt a kinship with this kindly man. He was someone to revere.

Hour after hour I would watch and he would struggle. He would pick and he would shovel. He would dig and he would scrape. He would wince when he would bend or turn. He would grunt as he would stand. You could see it in his sunken eyes. The toll that it was taking. Open sores and beads of sweat. Calluses and cramps. You could see the strain and feel the pain of his muscles and his tendons. He was exhausted by his labor. He had little more to give. Dick was sixty-nine years old. Give or take a year. I was young so he looked old. However old he was. His wrinkled face and weathered skin are etched into my brain. Darkly tanned and thick and tight from hours in the sun. He had swollen hands and knuckles and a slightly curving spine. It was a poignant revelation of life coming to an end.

Dick was proud. The man worked hard. He did all that he was asked. He labored for his daily bread. He gave more than he took. And, on that day in our backyard, my mother fed him well. Meat and bread and homemade wine. Olives, cheese and grapes. For him it was a banquet. For my mother it was sparse. It was basic food but filling. It was compassion on a plate.

What stays with me, however, was his eloquence and grace. He would always thank my mother as she offered him his lunch. He would take her hand and kiss it as a sign of his respect. He would dust his clothes and wash his face then find a place to sit. But before he touched a piece of food, or a single crumb of bread, first he prayed to heaven for the bounty he received. He put his plate beside his shovel and he dropped-down on his knees. He removed his cap and held it to his heart against his chest. He was grateful for the brief repast as frugal as it seemed. He was thankful for the strength he had to work another day. No mention of his struggle. No bitterness or anger. Only prayerful thanks and gratitude for the life that he endured.

Dick was pious and monastic. He was lifted by his faith. He was a rock. He was a flower. He could be delicate or hard. He was a man of modest dignity. He was profound in many ways. He was prepared to meet his maker. To be taken from this world. To be carried by the Seraphim on the wings of his own prayers. To the Kingdom of the faithful for whom his bell would toll. Three times a day, the Angelus, to commemorate his life.

CHAPTER 6
SIDNEY

The first job that I ever had was with Sidney "Shep" LaCove. A part time gig. A warehouse job. A stock boy and a clerk. It wasn't much to speak about but it got me through the week. Some pocket change but not much more. At least I didn't have to think. I never called him Sidney. He was always Shep to me. On occasion someone called him Sid but they didn't know him well. Those of us who knew him well would only call him Shep.

My father brought him home one day. For dinner I believe. For antipasti and spaghetti. For some wine and homemade bread. A stranger then. Not yet a friend. We took him in and fed him well. It was not at all unusual for my father to be gracious. To take a stranger in at night. To invite them home for dinner. It was common for my father to be hospitable and kind. He had learned this from his parents and I have learned the same from mine. It echoes the tradition of a village near Cosenza. From a province in Calabria in the city of Nicastro. It was the birthplace of his father. It was the town where he was raised. In the south of rural Italy. On a hill above the sea.

The people there were Christians. They were provincial Roman Catholics. They were superstitious but religious. They were faithful and devout. The friars and the bishops and the monks and all the priests had insisted that the Son of God would return to them some day. The second coming of the Savior. A second chance to make things right. When Christ appears, the scripture says, he will be a stranger in your midst. A man in need. An innocent. A beggar on the street. And who would know the Son of God if they met him on the road. Would they take him in and feed him? Would they clothe and keep him warm? Would they prepare a meal of substance or would they turn the man away?

I wouldn't know the Son of God if he were standing on my foot. And that is why the proverb held such power over us. The very act of kindness to a stranger on the street was a reflection of our culture. Of our Faith and our belief. That is why the people of the villages and mountains took you in if you were hungry. If you were lost or passing by. For all they knew you could be Him. Incarnate Jesus Christ.

My dad met Shep in Pittsburgh. On Fifth Avenue. Uptown. He was a distributor. A merchant. A purveyor he had known. Wholesale goods and trinkets and cheap imported junk. Novelties and baubles by the carton or the truck. He sold lava lamps and bamboo mats. He sold sequin bags and hats. He sold plastic frames with cardboard prints of JFK and Lincoln. He sold everything and anything if he could make a buck.

At different times throughout his life he moved from town-to-town. He owned parking lots and vending carts. He ran bingo halls and bars. He had concession stands in dime arcades. He played the ponies. He played cards. He had been a boxer and a bouncer but you would never know it then. He was the rarest of the rarest breed and he was tough to figure out. He was illiterate but thoughtful. He was polite as he was crude. He was hard as nails but smooth as silk and he was devoted to his mother. He was a man of many faces and a man of many lives.

He was a man that I knew very well but really not at all. He was guarded. He was private. He was careful with his words. He would talk about the lives he led or the life that he was living. He would question where the years had gone and lament the time he'd lost. He seemed always in a hurry with no place else to go.

Shep LaCove was Jewish but he denied it out of spite. His father was a German Jew. His mother French and Catholic. He never tried to reconcile nor cared to make the effort. The name LaCove is French of course and he took it from his mother. It was her maiden name. Her given name. Her family name in Europe. His father's name I never knew and he would never once discuss it. He resisted every thought of him and he was indignant if you asked. He resented every single day the man who put them out. His mother and his brother and the infant Sid LaCove.

Fatherless and penniless. Homeless and deprived. This stayed with him. And haunted him. And tormented him for years. The poverty of childhood. The father never known. No family but the three of them. No traditions to observe. No faith that could sustain him and no interest in the truth. Burdened by his memory he cursed his father's life.

Shep would always move around. Sometimes year-to-year. Just as he would settle-in he would pack and move again. A building sold. A building burned. He lost his lease or lost his temper. Whatever caused the exodus he never stayed for long. The buildings that he occupied were clones of one another. They were dirty, dark and dingy and they grew smaller with each move. They were further up The Avenue and further off the street.

The first of all his buildings was the best place that he rented. It was large and it was sprawling and it faced the street below. Fifth Avenue. The Avenue. As it was always known in Pittsburgh.

But the entrance to this building, to his business and his shop, was not on Fifth or Chatham Streets but the alley in the back. A narrow little passage between Chatham and Magee. Parallel to Forbes and Fifth or somewhere in between. It was a loading zone. A shipping dock. It was a door beside a ramp. It sounded good when he would say that his business was on Fifth. But in reality it wasn't. That was merely a façade.

CHAPTER 6

The windows in his office at the back of this old building were tall and wide and spacious where you could view the street below. It was Fifth Avenue at Center and you could see for twenty blocks. We watched people come and people go. We watched the cabbies drop their fares. We saw limos with celebrities. We saw the circus come to town. But mostly we would watch parades. We loved the pageantry and color. As fate would have it, happily, we had a panoramic view.

It was the starting point for all parades. Where floats would come to gather. It was the high command. The battle zone. The center of the storm. It was a fabulous location and we never once got wet. We were dry and we were cozy on our perch above the street. No crowds to block our jaded view. No fear of rain or snow. No pushing for a place to sit. And food enough to eat. We had a bathroom and binoculars. We had privacy and perks. We had everything we needed and got anything we asked.

When people saw us at the window looking down at all the chaos they would wave and they would whistle and they would point at us and yell. Some invited us to join them on the street beside the vendors. Some of them were schmoozing as a way to get inside. But we were spoiled rotten. We had it much too good. So we waved and nodded sheepishly and pretended not hear.

We sat and waited patiently. We watched it all unfold. Flowered floats and dancing bears. Horses, dogs and mimes. Large balloons of every shape. Every color. Every size. Marching bands in uniforms with tassels, bells and stripes. Confetti fell like snowflakes as it scattered in the wind. Streamers fell and banners hung. Batons were twirling like propellers. They were blazing red and brilliant blue. They were pink and orange and yellow. They were emerald green and lavender with stripes and squares and circles. The more colorful the rainbow the more jubilant the crowd.

Pennants flew and parents smiled and children laughed and gig-
gled and with every wave and every cheer the anticipation grew. The
Shriners and the Mummers wore exotic feathered costumes. With
sequin hats and silver beads. With flourishes and bangles. They
blew their whistles and their sousaphones. They played cymbals,
chimes and drums. They danced and spun and bounced and
jumped. And the tempo was frenetic.

There were acrobats and astronauts and celebrities and firemen.
People hung from poles and lampposts just to cop a better view.
There were vendors on the corners selling hot dogs, fries and pret-
zels. They sold taffy covered apples and corn dogs on a stick. They
had cocoa for the children. They gave coffee to the parents. They
made cider in a barrel and they served it from a tap.

From where we sat above the crowd it was animated bedlam.
Floating heads and armless hands waving in the air. Hats were bob-
bing up and down without bodies to support them. The sidewalks
seemed to be alive. They were organic and amorphous. The crowd
all breathed and sighed and cheered in one collective voice.

Balloons were bouncing everywhere each tugging at their strings.
Some were anchored to the children. Some were tethered to a stick.
Some escaped captivity and spiraled out of sight. Past the street
lamps and the brick veneer and the window where we sat. Some
slowly passed and drifted by. Almost leisurely at will. While others
seemed to ricochet and carom off the glass. Regardless of the
season, because the weather didn't matter, we never missed a
pageant or a major holiday. Easter and Thanksgiving. Labor Day and
Christmas. July the Fourth. St. Patrick's Day. Columbus Day or New
Years. We were there for all of them. And Shep was there for us.

Then something quite unthinkable. The landlord pulled his lease.
Unexpectedly and suddenly. More quickly than he thought. Shep
was forced to leave utopia and to find another place. A bridge too far.

CHAPTER 6

A dream deferred. A valley far less green. A new location somewhere else. A consolation prize.

The second of these venues left much to be desired. The building he would occupy, unlike our lofty perch, was dim and dark and seedy. It was abandoned and unkempt. It had no character of any kind. No potential for renewal. But worst of all it had no view. The parade had passed us by.

I drove that block not long ago and it was sad to see what happened. They dismantled every brick and stone and hauled them all away. Every trace of its existence, and every memory that I cherished, was vaporized and pulverized and buried in the ground. They treated with indignity any effort to preserve it. There is nothing left of value and no record of the past. Just some construct that replaced it. An edifice. A shell. A pink and gray and polished block. Uninviting and austere. Prefabricated panels of aluminum and steel. Cold and flat and linear and completely unappealing. It is relentlessly offensive to the buildings which embrace it. No regard for continuity or historic preservation. It is a monumental vision of some avante-architect who tried to marry Frank Lloyd Wright with Gropius and Bauhaus. It has no character or feeling. It has no memory or soul. It has no function but pretentiousness. It is ego run amuck.

This district with the wholesale vendors stretched for many blocks and Shep LaCove knew all of them from one end to the other. He knew them and they knew him by their first names and their last names. He knew their married names and maiden names. He knew their nicknames and their surnames. And if he didn't like your given name he would bestow one of his own. Mr. Slinky was the name he gave to a carnival contortionist. The coroner was Mack the Knife and there was an armless guy named Lefty. His landlord's name was Murray but he always called him Money and Cue Ball was the bald guy who sold papers on the street. Shep had names for everyone but he called his bookie Sir.

He knew the junkies on the corner and the dealers that supplied them. He knew the hookers and the lawyers but had little use for either. He knew a handful of policemen and he always gave them something. Toys if they had children or a bracelet for the wife. He was smart enough to understand that he needed some protection and he encouraged them to hang around so their presence would be felt. He knew the bankers on The Avenue. The judges and the cons. The wealthy men and homeless girls from every walk of life. He felt comfortable with all of them and they trusted him as well.

His new place on The Avenue was musty, cold and dank. It was thick with dirt and slick with grease that was piling up for years. The oil and the sawdust and the shavings from the turbines were caked between the planking of the floorboards and the vents. An industrial machine shop had resided there for years. When it folded they just took their tools and left the sludge behind.

The storeroom reeked of disinfectant when the renovation was complete. He used chemical carcinogens to keep viruses at bay. He was paranoid of microbes. He feared rodents, germs and roaches. He slathered paint and pesticides by the quart and by the gallon. He feared everything from measles to bacterial infections. He cringed at just the passing thought of contracting some disease. He scrubbed and bleached and sanitized. He cleaned everything in sight. He signed a lease. Then hung a sign. Then went back to selling junk.

The warehouse was bulging with boxes and bundles. There were cartons and bottles and barrels and racks. He stocked cases of key rings that glowed in the dark and flashlights and T-shirts with slogans and quips. He sold everything with batteries and anything that flashed. The more it whorled and whizzed and whirred the more of it he stocked. I wondered who these people were who bought this goofy stuff. The Elvis lamps and leopard rugs. The kewpie dolls of Gandhi. The pencils and the fountain pens that played Yankee

Doodle Dandy. The Chia pets and plastic worms. The polyester suits.

Saturdays and holidays were as hectic as they come. Christmas week was hellish. Easter was a zoo. Hanukah was madness but Shep adjusted well. He enjoyed the pandemonium. The chaotic confrontation. It was unabated lunacy. A calculated risk. The people who surrounded Shep were very much like him. They were drifters. They were loners. They were living on the edge. He saw himself in some of them so he nurtured them as friends. He had a twisted way of seeing things that was impossible to grasp. He saw his life for what it was and he loved it warts and all.

Shep was their supplier and they needed what he sold so they came to him to buy his wares and then they hawked them on the street. The cars they drove were clunkers. They were aging rusted hulks. They drove station wagons, panel trucks, VW's and Pintos. They were more than transportation. They were offices on wheels. The hucksters packed their cars and trucks with tons of mindless trash and stacked them to the windshield. They were loaded front to back. They parked along the highway near a busy overpass. They traveled to the steel mills and the coalmines and the bars. They hit the beer joints and the taverns that were common in the sixties. The Dew Drop Inn. The Glory B. The Steel Curtain and The Huddle. They sat beside a parking lot where workers left their cars and twice a month they made this trek when payday rolled around. They knew that in the steel mills the Eagle flew on Friday.

They hustled football games and baseball games and basketball and soccer. They scouted church bazaars and carnivals and Little League and pool halls. They made their rounds and picked their spot. They took your cash and ran. They were frumpy and abrasive men who smoked really bad cigars and they rarely shaved or bathed or washed. You could smell them from your car. They were looking for your pity. They were aiming at your heart. They would make you feel uncomfortable or guilty or unkind.

So you would buy a pound of chocolate in the shape of Pennsylvania. Or a Rolex watch with precious gems that looked suspiciously like glass. Or the hat the Mazeroski wore when he hit his last home run. It didn't seem to matter that you were buying imitations. It looked like the original and it didn't cost as much. More than that you bought this crap to help the poor guy out. But nine times out of ten of course he wasn't poor at all. You had been conned. You had been hustled. You had been taken for a ride.

Not all of them were out for blood. Deceitful or dishonest. Some of them were desperate and they had no other choice. Those in need would hustle hard for their rent checks or their healthcare. They did it for the money or to buy their kids some clothes. Some hustled for the fun of it. Some did it for the booze. But most of them were shysters. They were heartless shallow men.

The same men in the rusted cars that met you in the alley would come to see old Sidney in a brand new Coup de Ville. They drove Cadillacs and Lincolns or Mercedes Benz sedans. They wore leather coats. Not flannel shirts. They wore expensive tailored suits. The con men worked the summer months and spent their winters in the sun. They lived in Tampa or in Boca with their girlfriends at their side. They had fancy cars and part time wives and spoiled brats for kids. They had everything that they could want. They lived a very healthy life. It was a sham. It was a scam. It was a shame. It was a game. It was a clever way to hustle and they never once got caught. The Wall Street brass and shyster cons share a basic rule of thumb. Buy it low and sell it high and rip the suckers off.

The new place on The Avenue seemed alien to me. The clientele was different and there were strangers on the street. Shep knew fewer of the newer crowd and he saw less of his old friends. There was a difference in the people and it didn't feel the same. It wasn't like the other place that he had rented down the block. That building had a history. A memory. A soul. It also had a deli with the best corn beef in town.

South Pittsburgh and Italian was as far as you could get from a restaurant known as Goldstein's in a Jewish neighborhood. I had never heard of matzos until I worked for Shep. Pastrami and gefilte fish had never passed my lips. Tripe and lox and bagels were a novelty to me. But I tried it and liked it and I couldn't get enough. Everything that Goldstein sold was freshly made by hand. He baked the bread and cured the beef. He made the mustard and the blintzes. He mixed the brine and pickle juice and packed them in a barrel.

I had never tasted food like that and I doubt I will again. Not because I haven't found more interesting cuisine but Goldstein's was a first for me so it will always be the best. It was the first time I had ever tried corned beef on the heel. On Jewish rye with mustard and with tomatoes and with lettuce. With coleslaw and a kosher dill. With seltzer from a bottle. It was the newness of that flavor that can never be replaced. It was the atmosphere at Goldstein's that gave that food its taste. The flavors were all new to me but their ethnicity was not. It was exotic but familiar. It reminded me of home.

There was an immigrant's attention to the making of that food. My father came from immigrants. My mother did as well. My mother made her own fresh bread. My father grew the garden. My mother's dad made homemade wine and my father's dad cured cheese. My aunts and uncles processed food. They pickled and preserved it. They raised and plucked their chickens. They made everything from scratch. The sauces and the pasta. The soups and all the sausage.

Goldstein made these things as well. With attention to detail. If God is in the details then this food was truly sacred. The consecration of the daily meal was the ritual of eating. Goldstein touched that sacred spot and I remember how it tasted.

The loading dock for Shep LaCove, and the kitchen of Sam Gold-stein, shared between the two of them a ceiling and a floor. On hot and humid summer days those odors filled the warehouse. One story down below the docks Sam's kitchen vented steam. Up it came, through cracks and pipes and gaps along the floorboards, and it drifted through the stockroom and the offices above. It permeated everything. Our clothes. The paint. The wood. But we couldn't close the windows and we wouldn't close the doors. We had no ventilation. No air-conditioned office. No heat exhaust. No cooling fan. Just a window and a breeze. The sharpness of that awful smell that was coming from that kitchen was strong enough and foul enough to knock you on your ass. There were better days than others. But there were days much worse than that. It depended on the menu and the temperature outside. If the menu called for cabbage, and it was eighty-five degrees, then Shep and I would sit outside to keep from being sick.

I played the field for Shep LaCove. I was utility and back up. I was a chauffeur and a stock boy and a gopher and a clerk. I made pick-ups and deliveries and I bought the guy his lunch. I painted walls and patched the floors and did carpentry and cleaning. I waxed his car and loaded trucks. I did favors for his friends. I liked the man. The man liked me. He treated me quite well. But, as friendly and as giving and as kind as he could be, he could be difficult and moody, he could be stubborn and aloof. Like all of us he had his quirks. His peeves and peccadilloes. But one of them annoyed me more than any other foible.

I had to drive his car a lot. For delivery and pick up. But first I had to clean it from the front seat to the back. I washed the windshield and the dashboard. I swept the rug and brushed the seats. I used Lysol spray and Windex before I sat behind that wheel. It was a LeSabre Custom Buick that was burgundy and beige. It was a gas hog and a guzzler and it was always in the shop. It was only one of many cars that he would beat into the ground. Shep treated cars like Kleenex. They were meant to be discarded. He would buy them and abuse them and then throw away the keys. He had no respect for vehicles. A car. A bus. A truck. Whatever kind of thing he drove it died within a year. He never changed the oil. It would never be inspected. The tires were bald and out of round and the valves were never timed. He rarely had a license and he never paid his fines. He refused to buy insurance and he lied about his age.

I would drive him everywhere. He was hiding from the law. I would be the captain of the Starship Sid LaCove and he was Mr. Sulu. He would navigate the course. Our final destination was never really known. He would grunt and I would turn. He would belch and I would stop. He would point and I would follow. And it went on like this for miles. That was how he lived his life. In fits and starts and spurts. Shepski was a piece of work and he kept me on my toes.

Shep LaCove was muscular. He was husky and well built. He was round and squat but nimble. He was agile for his size. He was the Buddha of the Buick when I drove him in his car. He was a Jewish sumo wrestler. A dirigible with legs. He would fold his arms across his chest and rest them on his belly. He protruded like a pregnant wife about to drop a baby. And every time he took a breath his stomach would expand. He inflated to the breaking point. And I feared he might explode. He sat silently and vacantly. Half-conscious but awake. Expanding and contracting. Oblivious and bored.

We were waiting at a traffic light and I glanced across the seat and I noticed something very odd and it caught me by surprise. For a man his size his legs were short. They were stubby and foreshortened. They never really touched the floor. They just dangled from the seat. He wore pointed shoes on skinny legs that supported all that weight. They seemed frail and disproportionate compared to his physique. On rare occasions when he drove I wondered how he reached the pedals.

So if and when he drove his car, illegally of course, I paid a little more attention to his driving and his feet. The purpose of those tapered shoes revealed itself to me. He didn't wear them to be stylish. Or for comfort. Or for fit. He wore them to extend his foot by two or three more inches. The only thing that touched the brake was the tip of his left shoe. The pedal for the gasoline was barely just in reach. He arched his foot and tipped his toe until it slightly grazed the pedal. He stretched his leg and tapped his foot and grunted as he pushed. Painfully but gracefully he contorted every limb. He was the Baryshnikov of driving. The Nijinsky of the road. Shep could never drive a stick shift with a manual transmission. His little legs and baby feet could never press the clutch. So his cars were automatic and his shoes were oversized and he drove without a license until he wrecked or lost his nerve.

The thing that really irked me though. The habit that annoyed me. The reason that I cleaned the car before I sat behind the wheel. Shep would chew and gnaw and bite and spit when he would drive. Not pumpkin seeds or bubble gum. Not jerky or tobacco. But toothpicks made of balsa wood. Or match sticks in a box. He'd bite them off like candy bars and chew them to a pulp. Then spit them out on anything that happened in his way. No matter where he may have been. Especially his car. He left behind a spittle spray of masticated wood. It was his calling card. His trademark. It was an organic advertisement. 'Shep was here' and 'Shep was there' and 'Shep drove his car today'.

So the interior was spattered with regurgitated fiber. The dashboard and the floor mats and the windshield and the seats. It seemed to be a phobia. It was compulsive and obsessive. It may well have been from tension. Not a habit or a trait. But whatever may have triggered this unsanitary practice. It was disgusting and repulsive. It was a slimy mess to clean.

So even with the smell of it, and even in the heat, I was eager to get back to work and leave Shepski in the car. I could only take so much of this. The driving and the spitting. The enlightenment and wisdom of a navigating mystic. An expectorating woodchuck. A Munchkin at the wheel. The dangle-dance of Balanchine with pointy little shoes.

From the window on the second floor, in the office near the desk, I could see who came and went from Goldstein's Bar and Grill. Socialites in fancy cars. Gangsters with their henchmen. Politicians and their concubines. Judges and their bailiffs. Anyone who's anyone knew Goldstein and his sons. The Mayor and his Commissioner ate dinner with the Sheriff. Loan sharks and their bookies shared a table with police. Clerics blessed agnostics and they broke each other's bread. Baseball stars and quarterbacks were known to throw some dice.

On the wall beside each table – in the lounge and in the deli – hung photographs and autographs of legends of the past. There were posters of the truly great. There were trophies on the shelves. Uniforms and artifacts were displayed behind the bar. Goldstein celebrated greatness. The famous. The renown. He had known these men for many years. He knew some of them quite well.

Most of them were boxers and their trainers and promoters. There was Harry Grebb and Fritzy Zivic. Billy Conn and Jake LaMotta. There was Jersey Joe and Sugar Ray and Rocky Marciano. There was Patterson and Primo and Little Eddy Foy. Foy was not a boxer. He came from vaudeville and the stage. He was an actor in the movies. A thespian by trade.

But in the back of Goldstein's restaurant near an entrance to the kitchen – near a photograph of Dempsey and Joe Louis and Max Baer – hung a photograph of Sid LaCove in boxing trunks and gloves.

It was the irony of ironies. A twisted act of fate. A photograph of Sidney with the greatest of the greats. Shep LaCove, like Goldstein, was more than friendly with these men. He sparred with them. And they with him. He was good when he was young. He toured with them. He trained with them. He fought them in the ring. He lived to fight. He fought to live. He had no other trade. A crossing right from Sid LaCove could knock you through the ropes. It was his money punch that paid the bills. If they didn't hit him first. Shep could not take an upper cut. It left him numb and weak. His fist was hard and tempered but his chin was made of glass. It was weak and it was fragile and he never stood a chance. He had guts and he had stamina. He had talent and desire. He had a punch that shook you to the bone but it was never quite enough.

So there he sat one story up. Fifteen feet from glory. From a crowd that he knew very well. And a title never won. I never heard him once complain but I know it must have stung. To look at Shep as he was then you would never have imagined. Short and fat and overweight and badly out of shape. He smoked cigarettes and stogies. He wheezed with every breath. It was hard to picture Sid LaCove as anything but burly. But that photograph was flattering. A fighter in his prime.

His ring name wasn't Sidney though. It wasn't Shep or Kid LaCove. I can't remember what it was although he told me several times. It was Lucky this or Pinky that or Pasty some dumb thing. It was an Irish name if I recall. Or they may have called him Packy. Or was Packy West the same Bob Hope that entertained the troops? I can't remember what it was but Sidney was not Irish. Sidney, as a fighting name, just didn't cut the mustard. No pugilist on God's green earth would ever fight as Sidney. Lucky. Pinky. Patsy. It was all the same to me. But Sidney didn't like the name whatever name what ever name it was.

I understood his point of view and I understood his reason. Shep LaCove was no one's fool. He was streetwise. He was savvy. He could dish it out and take it. He would never walk away. He was a loner. Not a loser. He was a fighter to the end. A survivor in the purest sense. He always paid his dues. He lived week to week and hand to mouth and he gambled every day. The more difficult the circumstance the harder he would fight.

But Sidney had another side. A gentle side as well. A side to him that no one knew. It surprises even me. I knew Shep for many years. I thought I knew him well. He was kind to me. And generous. He was loyal to his friends. He had nothing much to live on. And he was tighter than a drum. But he never once denied a friend if they were hurting or in need. He was first in line and last to leave regardless of the hardship. And he never asked for anything in payment or in kind.

What I did not know amazes me. And I'm amazed I did not know. His mother, whom I never knew, was very much alive. When he spoke about his mother it was rare and it was brief. He spoke of her in passing. In the past tense if at all. He was secretive and private and tenaciously protective. He kept her in a nursing home. He provided for her needs. He spent every dime he ever made to feed and clothe and house her. He did anything he had to do to keep her in good health. But she died alone quite suddenly, one summer in the sixties, and it crushed him like a millstone when they buried her that day.

What I perceived to be a struggle in his day-to-day existence was the consequence of sacrifice, attentiveness and love. His mother never really knew how difficult it was. Had she known I'm certain she would never have agreed. But for Shep it was no hardship. It was his duty as her son. He was giving back what she gave him. A life. A chance. A home. These were the very things a mother's son would need when still a child. A homeless child and fatherless abandoned to the streets. Unselfishly she gave her love and he repaid her with affection.

Thinking back as I am now there were other signs as well. The shadow of another man. The searching of a soul. A Samaritan in hiding. A shepherd in the flock. The spirit of a lonesome child trying to reach out.

It was a Pennsylvania Christmas and the snow was deep and thick. The salt trucks and the road crews had been working through the night. There were snowdrifts on The Avenue and flurries in the air. The clouds were grey and angry and the wind was cold and wet. It was sharp and it was cutting as it scratched across your face. The banners on the buildings and the flags that flew at dusk would pop and crack and whip and twist and slap against the sky.

We closed the shop that holiday and walked across the street. To the parking lot near Chatham where I always parked his car. I parked it by the convent. St. Rosalia's School for Girls. I didn't think that anyone would bother with it there. He owned that lot. Or leased it. From the city or the county. He used the cash from parking cars to support his dying mother.

As we walked across Fifth Avenue and turned toward St. Rosalia's Shep stopped and put his hand up. He gestured to be still. He pointed back across street to Goldstein's Bar and Grill. I saw a woman with a long black shawl standing at the curb. She was bent and aged and not well dressed. She was timid, frail and weak. She looked cold and drawn and underfed and her eyes were sad and dark. Her face was pale and chapped and rough. She was uneasy and con-fused. She turned away and stumbled as she stepped along the sidewalk. She slipped across snow and ice then stopped to rest her feet. She tried to get inside the store but the vestibule was locked. The door was latched and bolted and the lamps were dimly lit. Gold-stein always closed his shop for Hanukkah and Christmas.

Outside the door. Beside the door. An evergreen was leaning. A barren tree and haggard. It was dry and sparse and brown. It stood sentry in the deli since the holidays began. Every year around this time Sam would trim a tree. A Christmas Tree for customers. For his patrons and their kids. The ornaments were edible. Fruits and nuts and bagels. And what shouldn't be ingested could be used to set the table. He tied napkins and utensils to the branches with red ribbons. He wrapped the tree with popcorn that had been strung into a garland. Every year he had a tree. At the entrance to his restaurant. For the regulars to see and taste. As a gesture of good faith.

But when the holidays were over. When the tree had depleted. Sam would salvage all the plastic ware then throw it in the trash. He leaned it on the wall. Beside the door. Outside the window. The garbage men would make their rounds and throw it on the truck.

So there it stood. The Christmas Tree. The symbol of the season. A token of abundance and of bounty and of grace. But the little food that still remained was frozen and decayed. Bagels blue with bread mold. Some apricots and figs. Strands of homemade popcorn and some tinsel in the pines.

She backed into the shadow of the building by the deli. She was cautious and attentive. She was watchful and discrete. Then suddenly she moved beyond the shadow of the wall. She glided and she shuffled and she stumbled to the tree. The brittle rags and plastic bags that were wrapped around her sandals would crackle on the frozen snow as she stepped gently on the ice.

Finally we realized what that woman had been doing. She was reaching for the evergreen. She was foraging for food. Pressing hard against the frozen ground she strained to gain momentum. She pushed and stretched and leaned and rocked from her tiptoes to her heels. Her short frail-frame and withered arms were defeating her attempts. She was diminutive and tiny. The tree was tall and wide. Still she struggled for a crust of bread. For some candy or a fig.

It was sad and it was painful. It was sorrowful to see. It affected
Shep so deeply that it took his breath away. I saw in him that little
boy whose mother was forsaken. Condemned to walk the streets at
night with her children in her arms. His past became the present and
he became that homeless child. He saw in her his mother and he fell
apart and cried.

He inhaled another cold deep breath and then slowly crossed the
street. Like a cat he moved unnoticed so she wouldn't turn and run.
When he reached her she was frightened. She pulled away and cow-
ered. Embarrassed by her plight perhaps she tried to hide her face.
But before she walked away from Shep he gently took her hand. He
gathered from the Tree of Life all that he could reach. He handed her
the meager meal. She wrapped it in her shawl. He talked to her and
hugged her. She smiled at him and wept.

I couldn't hear a word they said. I was frozen in my tracks. But
Shep was clearly moved by this. By something that she said. He
removed his coat and scarf and gloves. He draped her with his
jacket. He wrapped his scarf around her neck and offered her his
gloves. Then he reached into his pocket and took some money from
his wallet. He counted it and folded it and pressed it to her hand.
The woman sobbed and Sidney cried and then she shuffled on her
way. Through the snow and through the flurries to the corner near the
bank. She crossed The Avenue to Bennett Street. She turned and
disappeared.

Shep drove me home that somber night and not a word was said
between us. The snow had stopped and it was dusk. There was no
one on the road. The moon was bright but not quite full and the air
was crisp and cold. I could feel the freshly fallen snow collapse
beneath the tires. I could hear it move and shift and break as it
pressed between the treads. The emptiness I felt that night was
magnified by silence.

By the time that we arrived at home the street lamps cast their shadows. The dry night air was blowing no more stiffly than a breeze. But strong enough to catch the snow it tossed it from the branches. It filtered down and swirled around as it spiraled through the lights. There was a crystal veil of powdered snow that sparkled as it fell. A sterile urban winter scene. Pale and unromantic. It was a cold and harsh December night and I was glad to see it end.

SIDNEY

CHAPTER 7
THE PATIO

I never really knew the man but I remember how he looked. He was big and strong and tall and black and he could break a tree in half. He had an easy smile and hearty laugh that was exuberant and cheerful. It started in his belly and erupted like a bomb. His laughter was contagious and expressive and delightful and his body shook like Jell-O when he tried to hold it back.

He was a gentleman my father knew from Wylie Avenue. On 'The Hill' just east of Pittsburgh near Bigelow and Center. The immigrants from Italy and the blacks from on The Hill lived side by side for many years and they shared that neighborhood.

Mr. DePaul Smith was self-employed. He was dependable and prompt. He drove a dump truck painted apple red with big black doors and fenders. It was dented, scratched and battered and it sputtered and it chugged. It leaned sharply to the driver's side. The shocks were worn and broken. Snapped like twigs from hauling scrap and smashing into things. Wooden doors and two by fours were stacked behind the cab. Lashed and tied with rope and twine. Bound and nailed and screwed. The doors were cracked and dirty and they were painted different colors. They were used to brace the cargo when the truck was fully loaded. They looked like giant dominos. Blue and green and yellow. The truck like him was playful. Colorful and bold. An animated character. A Disneyesque cartoon.

Mr. Smith was in construction so he often tore things down. Abandoned slums or tenements. A diner or a bar. He knocked them down and chopped them up and hauled them all away. He sold the copper and the stainless steel. The aluminum and brass. He salvaged chandeliers and door knobs and panes of leaded glass. He restored the wood and cleaned the brick and sold them second hand.

He would stack his truck with radiators, furnaces and washtubs. Hot water tanks or

I-beams. Whatever he could haul. He would pack them tight and stack them high and they shifted as he drove. But the multi-colored wooden doors held them all in place. He used a canvas tarp to cover all the rubble and the refuse. He secured it with a long thick rope and tied it to the frame. He looped the line and twisted hard. He knotted all the ends. He pulled until the tension caused the doors to creak and bend. When the tarp was firmly fastened and the scrap was all secured he hung a large square yellow sign with bold hand painted letters. STAY BACK! it said, STUFF DO FALL OFF! Then down the road he went.

I do not recall the day we met but I do recall that name. An uncommon name with character. So easily remembered. He was the first black man I ever knew. A very kindly man. He provided us with wood and brick to build our patio. We met him at a Baptist church on the North Side of the city and he took us to a nearby site where he had demolished some old building. It was a time in early '63 or maybe '64 when Pittsburgh was expanding and construction was frenetic. It was exciting or depressing depending on your viewpoint since, to realize the vision of a Renaissance in Pittsburgh, we sacrificed its character. We altered the old landscape.

The Arena was the first design to splash against the skyline. A silver dome on concrete piers. An auditorium on steroids. The dome itself would open and retract against itself. But I can't remember more than twice that it ever really worked. Theoretically the city said it was advanced in its conception. It could be an open-air performance space or a self-contained arena. But it was ugly and imposing and it didn't fit the site. It had a whacky flying saucer shape. Metallic and convex. It could have been a tacky prop in a science fiction movie.

It was conceived as something modern but it seemed so out of place and it clashed against the buildings that were one by one replaced. It was built for basketball and hockey. And for tennis and for concerts. Frank Sinatra came to play there. And so did Pavarotti. Rock bands screamed their heavy metal wicked wild routines. Circuses and tractor pulls and motocross and skating. Convocations, benedictions and high school graduations filled the seats and paid the bills and justified its status.

It never fit its purpose and was an eyesore on The Hill but there it stood and still they played and there they came to gawk. Basketball has come and gone and tennis was a pipe dream. The hockey team is still around but the concerts were a joke.

The price we paid for these events, for rock 'n roll and hockey, was the loss of every local lounge and jazz joint on The Hill. Duke Ellington. Earl Garner. Charlie Parker and Joe Williams. Ella sang and Dizzy played before the night clubs all went bust. Anyone could climb The Hill to drink or socialize. Or to listen to the greatest jazz this world has ever known.

But the Civic Center project had supplanted all that talent and ninety some odd acres were leveled to the ground. The churches and the synagogues were forced to close their doors. The barbershops and grocers had to move across the river. The butcher and the soda jerks lost everything they had and Pittsburgh lost its spirit if not something of its soul. Ironically the circle is unbroken, in a way, because the Civic Center building has been leveled to the ground. The wrecking ball reclaimed its own and fate has intervened. Now they plan to turn back time. To replicate the past. To fabricate a neighborhood. To restore what has been lost.

On the other side of Pittsburgh across the Allegheny River they plopped Three Rivers Stadium for baseball games and football. The demand for men in spikes and cleats, for the Steelers and the Pirates, far out-weighed the meager needs of the people who were born there. Some of them descends of the founders and the settlers. From the Germans, Scotts and Irish who had come to build a city. The North Side was the homeland that they transplanted and created. All of which was sacrificed for a pitcher's mound and goal posts. The businesses were bought or sold or forced to move away and speculators took their homes for parking lots and tollbooths.

More than fifty thousand people and some twenty thousand cars had replaced the streets and alleys and the gardens and the yards. A lifetime of devotion to a community and workplace was obliterated senselessly for the sake of competition. Once a month for several months the teams would come to town. They would play their games then leave again for three weeks at a time. And for the privilege of some football game, played seven times a year, thousands had to lose their homes. Their businesses. Their jobs. That community of founders and of immigrants and workers were apparently expendable and few of them survived.

They moved because they lost their trade or because of eminent domain. A euphemism often used for confiscation or collusion. Not for utilities or railroad tracks. Not for roads or transportation. But for hash marks on a football field or a diamond in the rough. Expropriation was the city's way of getting what it wanted. Without conscious and with forced consent they condemned that neighborhood.

The old Forbes Field in Oakland was another classic blunder. It was a baseball field with thick green lawns and a panoramic view. The outfield grass was checkered green and the infield dirt was umber. The bases and the foul lines were bright and white and soft. And the dugout and the bullpen were so perfectly aligned that Elroy Face and Murtaugh could see each other and blink. No telephone or intercom. No golf cart or a mascot. Just one sharp glance across the field and the pitcher took the mound.

Forbes was always packed with fans from the box seats to the bleachers but it never seemed to hold enough to make the owners happy. They tore it down in '69 or '70 perhaps and they buried every trace of it except the wall in center field.

The baseball team and football team now shared some common ground. A communal field of Astroturf that was plastic and synthetic. There was no grass or cool fall breeze. There was no view beyond the bleachers. Electric lights and power lines cast shadows on the field. It was sterile and confining. It was closed and claustrophobic. It was a fishbowl filled with screaming fans and they were screaming to get out.

The land where old Forbes Field once stood is now a building with a courtyard. It was purchased by the college when they decided to expand. The only thing that still remains is the wall from center field. A brick and ivy sentinel that protects that hallowed ground. It pre-serves for us the memory of what happened in that park. The last home run that Babe Ruth hit went over that brick wall and Mazeroski won the pennant for the Pirates in the sixties. Clemente brushed against that wall when he ran across the outfield and every kid who owned a glove had dreams of playing there. Honus Wagner. Smokey Burgess. The infamous Ty Cobb. All of them had popped a fly or rounded into home.

But history and legacy could not triumph over money so they left the wall but took the park and gutted a tradition. It lasted only twenty years that artificial turf. Since Forbes was de-constructed and base-ball went synthetic.

They soon realized, paradoxically, that they never should have done it. Like the Civic Center project, on The Hill above the city, they tore it down and cleared the land to build another park. Not one but two new stadia. Two monuments to progress. One for baseball. One for football. One for all and all for one.

So in the middle of this rubble on a street I can't remember I was introduced to DePaul Smith in overalls and boots. He was picking through the bricks and beams that once supported joists and rafters. Before the building that it used to be collapsed around itself.

This was the birthplace of our patio. A pile of broken wood. The last remains of someone's home that was forced to move away.

We salvaged everything that we could use from the wreckage and debris. Some four-inch posts and wide oak beams. Some roofing planks and gutters. We took cobblestones and downspouts and a length of copper flashing. We took all the bricks that we could find and all the blocks that we could carry. And we used every piece of every scrap to build our patio.

There were tons of bricks and yards of planks. A dozen posts and beams. Caked with lath and plaster and corroded thick with rust. And DePaul Smith with burly arms and Jell-O-bellied laughter stacked and loaded all this stuff and drove it to our house.

For days and weeks and months it seemed we chipped and scraped and hacked. Through tiers of wood and piles of brick and pounds of twisted nails. My mother with her hair tied-back and goggles on her eyes would wrap a scarf around her mouth to keep from choking on the dust. The bricks were cleaned and shaped and brushed and soaked and scrubbed with water then we lined them up by color and by the flatness of the stone. We were trying to determine which side or edge to use so that the pattern in the brickwork would be continuous and even.

I say "we" but I mean dad. He directed all our efforts. He had decided on a pattern of interlocking zigzags that was bounded by a border of cobblestone and mulch. On weekdays in the afternoons my mother tried to manage. Between breakfast, lunch and dinner and providing for the kids. She sanded wood and cleaned the bricks. She pulled and hammered nails. She packed the clay and tamped it down with a heavy cast iron plate. She made it firm and flat and solid and she leveled it with sand. Then she stacked the bricks in piles of four to make them easier to carry.

When my father wasn't working he was crawling in the dirt. He struck the lines and set the posts and shaped each cobbled stone. He took the bricks that mother cleaned and began to form his pattern. He didn't need a drawing. He had it in his head. He started in the middle of the patio to be and he worked each brick symmetrically in alternating rows. Inside out and edge-to-edge the patio took shape.

When the foundation had been finished and the pattern was complete he built supports to brace the posts, and raised the rafters and the roof. Then he tarred the wooden planks and boards to protect it from the weather and planted annuals, perennials and rows of box shaped hedges. The hedges didn't last too long. They died before they grew. So he replaced them all with flower beds and a line of Rose of Sharon.

It took months of broken fingernails and calluses and blisters but finally the patio was christened and anointed. It was large and tall and spacious and it was pleasing to the eye. It was very well constructed. It was very often used.

I was amazed that, only months before, it was nothing more than rubble. A heap of wood and bricks and nails destined for the junkyard. My father had the vision to see treasure in a scrap heap. So he sanded, scraped and cleaned it, and he willed it back to life.

And DePaul Smith with barrel chest and Jell-O-bellied laughter carried, stacked and hauled that stuff and delivered it with pride. Piece by piece and plank-by-plank a pavilion was constructed and DePaul Smith, that lovely man, gave us more than he could know. It changed its form and shape and style and structure over time but still it stands behind that house on Dagmar Avenue.

That was only the beginning of the cookouts and the picnics. The parties and festivities. The frivolity and fun. We roasted chickens on an open spit and barbecued some spare ribs. We grilled shish kabob and sausage that my mother made from scratch. My uncles came to visit on the weekends in the summer. To drink some wine and harmonize and sing their favorite songs.

The patio was many things as it grew to meet our needs. It was a bunkhouse and a fortress. A clubhouse and a den. It was second base and center field. It was a goal post and a dugout. We told stories we built bonfires and we nearly burned it down. Whatever need that we might have would be the need that it fulfilled. It was a vital part of growing up. An inanimate companion. It was a playmate and a confidant when there was no one else around.

Our backyard was our playground. It was our private field of dreams. It was the meeting place for any kid who played any kind of sport. We played whiffle ball and football. We played bocce and badminton. We played horseshoes, dodge ball, hide and seek. We played shuffleboard and darts.

The yard was small but big enough for teams of five or six. Home plate was a floor mat that we had taken from a car. A grayish Plymouth Belvedere that belonged to Mr. Porter. He didn't know we took it and we never gave it back. The maple tree behind home plate was the backstop for the pitcher. And first base was a broken stone that stuck out from the wall. A sloping wall of cobblestone planted thick with ivy. And with sedum and with myrtle to hold the dirt in place.

The corner of the patio was second base and center, and third base was a Frisbee that had lost its will to fly. Since the corner of the patio was also second base then center field was underneath the patio enclosure. If the ball went through the infield and rolled past second base then the fielder had to dodge the post when he was running for the ball. More than once I whacked my head or smacked my shin our shoulder. No matter where it landed you had to chase the ball. And you had to be prepared to bleed when you ran through center field. There was no such thing as out of bounds or an automatic homer.

The only time a game was called was when the ball sliced sharp to right. That would be the death knell and we could kiss the ball good-bye. To the right side of the patio lived a man named Harry Bondi. Beyond the yard beside our house. Above the wall behind a fence. Mr. Bondi was our neighbor and I use that word with caution. He lived behind our family home for more than twenty years. He was unpleasant and unhappy. And he took it out on us. And he always seemed to be around when we were playing ball.

The sloping wall of cobblestone was filled with gravel and debris and it ran the length of our back yard from one end to the other. That wall of stone was put there for stability and strength. To hold the soil to the hillside. To prevent the hill from sliding. It was divided in the middle. Half was Bondi's. Half was ours.

At some point Mr. Bondi ran a fence above wall with two inch slats and chicken wire and metal posts and brambles. It was an eye sore from the very start and he never did maintain it. He discarded weeds and grass and stones and he threw them down the hill. They were out of sight from up above from the widows of his house but the rocks and twigs and other junk were landing in our yard. It took years of constant bickering to have him to clean that mess and even then my parents did the weeding and the planting.

Harry Bondi was a cynic and a very lonely man. A curmudgeon and an ogre. A widower. A Scrooge. He was short and fat and bald and crude and a nuisance to the neighbors and God-forbid a baseball ever landed in his yard. He kept every ball we ever hit. No matter what it was. A softball or a baseball or a tennis ball or birdie. He never once returned a thing. Not once in twenty years. Except when he was dying and he was forced to leave his home.

He grew too old to care about a silly baseball game and he grew too frail to shake his fist and chase our errant fouls. But when he moved into his sister's home and he sold his old brick house he gave us back a treasure trove of more than thirty balls.

They were rotted, stained and molded in a damp and dirty sack and the stitches were unraveled or snapping at the seam. They were useless wads of string and twine but we took them nonetheless because this random act of kindness was something genuine and rare. We knew that he was very sick and we sensed that he was dying so we accepted with humility this sack of putrid stuff. We accepted it for what it was. A departing act of grace. But Bondi lived for many years and his sister died instead.

We weren't always quite as gracious in those years when we were neighbors. Retaliation was a common theme between Bondi and the kids. One year in the summer, before I turned thirteen, a friend of mine named Gary had a brand new Spalding ball. It was spotless and immaculate with bright red chevron stitching. The lettering was stamped in black and it was 'signed' by Mickey Mantle. When he threw the ball across the yard I could hear it coming toward me. I could see it as it hit my glove and I could feel it burn my skin. My glove was smooth and tight and firm. It smelled of saddle soap and cowhide. So I pulled it out and threw it back and it cracked against his mitt.

My father bought a station wagon seven days before. From Pascoe Ford in Bridgeville. In 1964. And the ball, just like that Galaxie, had a smell and feel to it. The cowhide and the Naugahyde. The rosin and the Windex. It was the first new car we ever owned. It was burgundy or plum. The leather seats were shiny black and the dashboard matched the rugs. It was the nicest car we ever owned and it never once broke down. We washed it and we waxed it. It reflected in the sun. The paint job was metallic so it shimmered in the rain and the roof rack, which was polished chrome, refracted like a prism.

The next car that my father bought was in 1968. Yet another Galaxie. A wagon like before. It was turquoise blue with black bench seats but it should have been bright yellow. It was a lemon from the very day he drove it from the showroom. And things got worse from that day on until the damn thing nearly killed me.

The motor mount had broken off while I was driving to the drug store and when it did the engine block shifted to the right. When the engine dropped and shifted the accelerator jammed and it pulled the pedal to the floorboard and I couldn't make it stop. I tried to shift it into neutral but nothing seemed to happen. The linkage had been broken when the engine dropped and twisted. I pulled the keys from the ignition on the column by the gearshift but still the engine screamed and burned and pushed me down the hill.

I ran the stop sign crossing Sebring and another at Bayonne. I sped hopelessly down Fallowfield past Harry Bondi's house. I had both feet on the power brake and the keys were in my lap. The gearshift dangled uselessly and the parking brake was locked. From Fallowfield I bounced and sparked and screamed like bloody murder. I was heading toward a hairpin turn near Crane and Gladdis streets. I blew through stop sign after stop sign and I nearly hit a school guard.

I tried desperately to slow the car by staying in the gutter. I hugged the curb and held the wheel. I pulled tightly toward the sidewalk. I was hoping for blowout. I was looking for a ditch. I turned sharply onto Dagmar as I rounded one last bend. Then suddenly. Amazingly. The Galaxie imploded. The engine hissed and sputtered. The radiator belched. The engine block had frozen and the pistons popped a cork.

I stopped the car or it stopped me less than fifty feet from home. And I ran across my uncle's yard and sprawled across his lawn. My heart was pounding loud enough to rupture my own eardrums. I was sweating like a racehorse and I couldn't catch my breath. That turquoise lemon memory still haunts me in my dreams. I don't know how I made it home or ducked the Reaper's scythe.

There were two of us that sunny day. Just Gary and myself. Running fast and tossing hard like DiMaggio and Koufax. We threw the ball and spun around and caught it on the fly. We jumped and dove and scooped and trapped and threw it back and forth. We skimmed the grass and muffed a catch but it never hit the ground. We felt like big league players on the outfield in Forbes Field but we were nothing more than amateurs chasing down our dreams.

I tossed one more curving stinging pitch and Gary caught it in the web. Then he pulled his glove and grabbed a bat and pointed at the sky. He was warning me to back away. But he wanted me to catch it. So I moved closer toward the outfield beyond the patio and wall.

"I'll pop-it-up to center", he forewarned me from the plate. Then he lobbed the ball and swung the bat and whacked it hard and fast. It clicked against the cowhide like a Spanish castanet and it echoed as it drifted past the entrance into Hades. I could hear him gasp from where I stood but there was nothing we could do. By the time that he had climbed the fence Bondi had the ball.

The dog was barking frantically and the old man shook his fist and Gary tried to plead his case but Bondi sneered and cursed. He threatened him with trespass and he said he'd call the cops. Or worse he'd sick the dog on him to bite him on the ass.

The dog was just like Bondi. Grouchy. Fat and short. It was a boxer or a bull dog that slobbered when it barked. It had drooping jowls and pigeon toes and a tuft of bristled hair. Like a porcupine or rodent with a collar and a chain. Like a Munchkin with an attitude and a pudgy little face.

Gary couldn't tell his father because he never should have been there. He was grounded several weeks ago for skipping out of school. And the Spaulding was a birthday gift. Not to him but to his brother. He was a seething angry lunatic and he wanted some revenge but he didn't know what he should do so he took his glove and left.

We didn't talk for two more days. And then I saw him on the street. He was walking with his neighbor's dog and he was carrying a bucket. It was a yellow plastic children's pail with a little matching shovel. My sister used to play with one. In a sandbox. Or the beach. He followed cautiously behind the dog with that bucket in his hand and he waited for that mixed breed pooch to do what all dogs do. I was astonished as he scooped it up and put it in his bucket and that is when he saw me and he laughed and waved goodbye.

Later in the evening he called me on the phone. He asked if I would meet him on the patio that night. He told me that he had a plan and that the plan involved revenge. I knew that it was Bondi by the anger in his voice. So I promised not to say a word. I agreed to be his scout.

I met him on the patio at ten o'clock that night. It was dark and it was quiet. He was somber and reserved. The evening and his attitude were perfectly aligned. He handed me a package and he told me not to squeeze it. He told me not to drop it or it place it in my lap. He had taken all the contents of that bucket he had carried and he dumped it in a paper bag and tied it with a string.

He had some sparklers and some duct tape and a can of something slimy. He taped the fireworks to the paper bag and then he smeared it all with goop. It was the lubricant his father used to grease the axle on his truck. He had mixed it with some Vaseline and a marinade of Crisco.

When he had finished his concoction and he had smoked his cigarette he slipped around the broken fence and shimmied up the hill. He crawled along the bramble-brush and he ran across the yard then quickly he was on the porch and kneeling by the stoop. He put that sack of dog dirt in the center of the landing then lit the fuse and rang the bell and then ran into the bushes.

The paper bag ignited and the fireworks popped and spit and Bondi ran around the house shrieking like a banshee. He ran along the banister and leapt across the porch and when he did he landed hard and stepped in all that shit. He squealed and swore and stomped and yelled. He threatened and he cursed. But the more he did his doo-doo dance the more havoc that it wreaked.

The contents and the lubricant were propelled in all directions. It adhered to every surface and it stunk like what it was. It stuck like glue to everything. His pants. His shirt. His shoes. It launched itself across the deck. It spattered on the window. And just when things had settled down, and the fireworks had subsided, around the porch and up the steps leapt that yappy little dog.

Barking and biting and snapping and sniffing. Spinning and bouncing and chasing his tail. Dumber than a doorknob it ran across the porch and right into the middle of that slimy slurry mess. It spun again and lost control then slid right off the porch. Bondi was beside himself and Gary wet his pants.

I watched this from the patio, and I knew it wasn't right, but still I laughed at both of them and still I laugh today.

THE PATIO

CHAPTER 8
1966

In the summer of my early teens, as I prepared to make my way, I was an adolescent rebel and I didn't have a clue. When the future was as distant as the planets from the sun and choices were for those who seemed to know where they were going. I came to learn, quite early on, that my fate was not my own. Not then at least. Not there I thought. Not in that place and time. My journey was beginning and my life was yet to come.

I saw myself a caterpillar weaving a cocoon. Wanting to be more a butterfly and straining to break free. I thought school to be a nuisance back in 1966 because it kept me from so many things that I wanted more to do. From sailing on the Chesapeake to canoeing the Zambezi. Or riding in a box-car on a train to Istanbul. Railroad tracks and blacktop roads were luring and hypnotic. Paddle wheels and ferry boats were waiting at the dock.

These were the symbols of adventure and of freedom that I cherished. Kuralt was on the road again and I wanted to be him. Lowell Thomas was my hero. Machu Picchu was my goal. Richard Leaky. Marco Polo. Amundsen and Peary. Howard Carter. Lord Carnarvon. Elgin and his marbles. I admired them for the lives they lived and I wanted some adventure. I was inquisitive and curious but equally naïve. The Oracle of Delphi. The ruins of Pompeii. The Megaron of Minos and the Palace of Shapur. Herculaneum. Vesuvius. Meteora and Mount Athos. Asia Minor. Katmandu. And the via Dolorosa.

I planned to visit all of them and I intended to explore. Archaeology and history had captivated me. I was Samuel Langhorne Clemens before he knew Mark Twain. I was the dreamer of a vision that was waiting to be seen.

I once considered leaving home in 1966. Packing up my duffle bag and heading out to sea. I decided that a merchant ship might be the way to go. To the Navy or the Coast Guard. To some mercenary crew. The world that I was searching for would splash against the bow. The waves would break and scatter and they would smack me in the face. I would go to where the oceans touched the land that they surrounded. Where the Atlantic and Pacific and the Indian would meet.

Every waterway and inlet. Every port and fjord and bay. Every gulf and every blue lagoon would carry me ashore. They would lead me to their villages. To their rivers and their lakes. To the Yangtze of the Orient or the Ganges of the Faithful. To the tropics of the Amazon or the pharaohs of the Nile. To the Volga and the Tiber and the mighty Mississippi. To the Zuider Zee. The Grand Canal. To the Rio de la Plata.

I would visit every speck of land beyond the next horizon. Every peak and every valley. Every mountain. Every stream. Every inch of terra firma. Every road that led to Rome. Or to Athens or to Leningrad. Or to Senegal or Bali.

I decided that adventure was the only job I wanted. I would travel. I would wander. I would learn languages and cultures. I would investigate the planet from Galapagos to Guam.

But it never once occurred to me that I might have been too young. That my dreams were too ambitious back in 1966. That life would have to take its course. That adventure had to wait. That the life I lived was tethered by the father to the son. And my father chose to change my course in 1966. He explained to me the need to learn.

To appreciate my brain. That, those men whom I admired so much, were educated men. They studied stellar constellations and positions of the moon. They navigated back-and-forth by looking at the sun. They calculated equinox and charted their own courses. They were cartographers, geographers, astronomers and captains. They knew alchemy and botany. Biology and science. Most of them could read and write and all of them could think.

My father knew far better, much better than I knew, that learning is discovery, adventure and escape. That, in order to appreciate the travel that I planned, I had to be prepared for life. I had to learn to think. I had to know where I was going or it wasn't exploration. That discovery was meaningless without knowing what it meant.

So, in light of this, the next four years were narrowly defined. My path had well been chosen and I knew where I was going. I took the road most traveled - unlike Emerson or Frost - that led me to a private school and to a cloistered education. It was parochial and formal. A respected institution. It was regulated. Regimented. Demanding and confined.

One did not choose to go there, you were chosen to attend. It was selective and solicitous. Small but unpretentious. Neither privileged nor affected. Just competitive and firm. It was inflexible and rigorous but you were given what you earned. It was insular and prudish and admitted only men. Women would have kept us from our studies and our mission. They would have tempted our libidos and destroyed the will to learn. We were there for knowledge and for discipline and faith. No distractions from the outside world were tolerated there.

But, before they would accept me from a common public school, I would need to prove my worthiness. I would need to be prepared. So, in that summer of transition between puberty and freedom – when I would rather have been Darwin on the Beagle out at sea – I was given books to read and verse to contemplate. I had to demonstrate some basic skills in reading comprehension. I wrote book reviews and summaries of story lines and subplots. I analyzed antagonists, protagonists and heroes. I studied grammar and declension and I conjugated verbs. I tried desperately to earn my seat. It was not given to you then.

June, July, and August were such solitary months. I was alone and I was lonely. I was restricted to the house. I had a compass and a slide rule for geometry and math. A notebook and a work sheet and a list of twenty books. No diversion from the task at hand. No time for making friends. No concept of a life beyond the room I occupied.

The companions that I did have were conjured and imagined. Pudd'n Head and Ethan Frome. Billy Budd and Dodger. Antigone. Persephone. Oedipus the King. Sophocles. Euripides. Aristophanes and Plato. Hemingway and Shakespeare. The Brothers Karamazov.

There were princes and paupers and one-legged whalers. There were mystical women and mythical men. There were soldiers of fortune and robbers and villains who lived by their wits and the tip of their swords. They lived tragedies and comedies and ironies and dramas. They spoke soliloquies and monologues and dialogue and verse. I read about the universe from the Big Bang to the Quasars and dabbled in philosophy and the history of Man.

As much as I resented these demands of supplication – the guidelines and the deadlines and the rules that were applied – still I did what I was asked to do. I read each book and play. I interpreted and analyzed and submitted my reports. I will admit that I was anxious and resisted more than once. I would have chosen otherwise had my father not insisted. My friends were scattered everywhere and none of them would join me. So I relented and attended as if I really had a choice.

My life of course is richer now for the choices that I made. Either choices of my own design or those imposed when I was young. For the effort that I mustered. For the brain food that I ate. For the father who believed in me before I knew my fate. Before the dream I had envisioned as the life that I would lead, became the life that I am living and the future that I see.

When I think about my life right now, and the course it might have taken, I owe my heart and mind and soul to 1966.

EPILOGUE

In the time that it took me to complete this manuscript, I not only lost my father, Alfred Michael, but my mother Isabel Rose and my older brother Alfred Paul.

For me, the significance of the dedication to my father in the opening pages of this memoir is ever more meaningful and profound – *senza memoria vita non esiste.*

For the reader let this be an invitation to live every moment, embrace the ones you love and to recognize that, without memory, life does not exist.

Your memories become you.

RFV